WHO'S ALLOWED TO PROTEST?

ALSO BY BRUCE ROBBINS

The Beneficiary

Atrocity: A Literary History

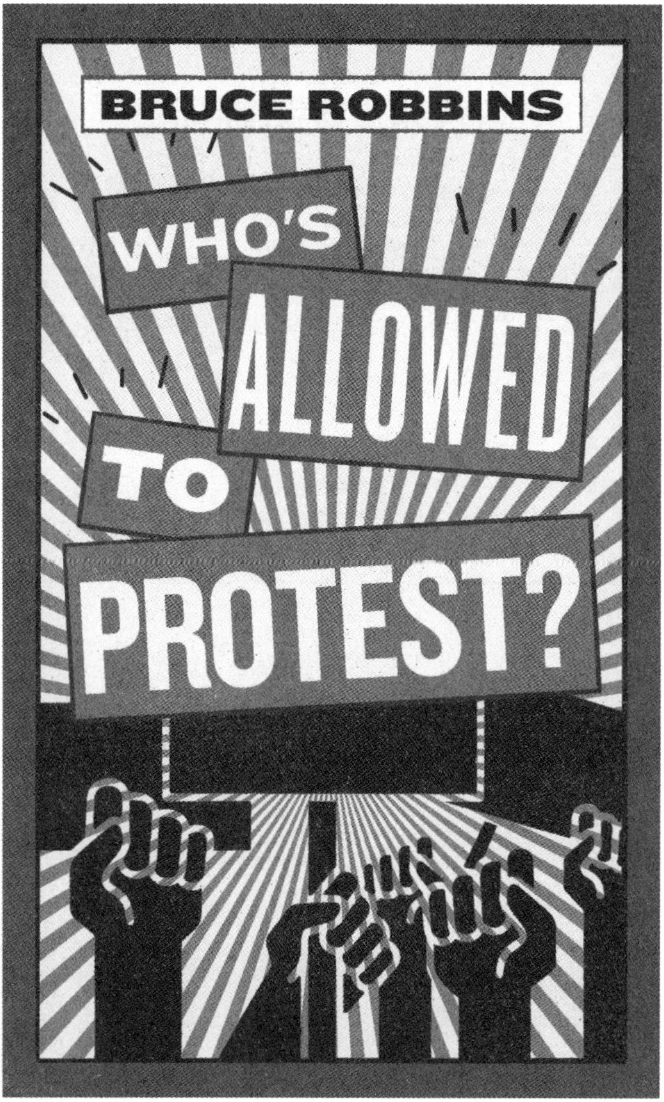
BRUCE ROBBINS
WHO'S
ALLOWED
TO
PROTEST?

MELVILLE HOUSE
BROOKLYN • LONDON

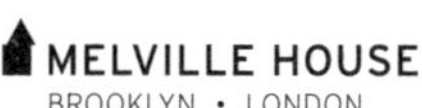

WHO'S ALLOWED TO PROTEST?

First published in 2026 by Melville House

First Melville House Printing:
Distributed by Penguin Random House LLC, 1745 Broadway, New York, NY 10019 USA. www.penguinrandomhouse.com

Melville House Publishing
46 John Street
Brooklyn, NY 11201
and
Melville House UK
Suite 2000
16/18 Woodford Road
London E7 0HA

mhpbooks.com
@melvillehouse

ISBN: 978-1-68589-257-9
ISBN: 978-1-68589-258-6
(eBook)
Library of Congress Control Number: 2025948130

Printed in the United States of America
1 3 5 7 9 10 8 6 4 2

A catalog record for this book is available from the Library of Congress

CONTENTS

PROLOGUE

"ENTITLED CHILD EXPECTS TO EAT LUNCH EVERY DAY. GIRL LITERALLY WANTS FOOD TO BE HANDED TO HER ON A PLATE"[1]

I probably have too much faith in history, meaning faith in the likelihood that history's arc, though long, will eventually be forced (by our combined efforts, each of them tiny and trivial and apparently meaningless) to bend toward justice. At Columbia University, where I teach, the administration celebrated with unmistakable pride, in 2018, the fiftieth anniversary of the world-historical student protests of 1968. That had not been their reaction fifty years earlier. The things said and done in the fifty years in between had made a difference. Of course, by 2024, six years after the anniversary, the people in charge at Columbia did not seem to have been briefed on the pride that was supposedly now the official line. This time round, the university president's response to a new wave of protests was swifter and harsher than it had been in 1968. Still, the fact remains that by 2018, history had brought the administrators to acknowledge, at least for public consumption, a less law-and-order sense of what a protest demanded, morally speaking. Since the days when a predecessor administration called in the police to empty the occupied buildings and crack student heads, there had been a shift in moral vision—that has to be said, even if that shift turned out to have no practical effects. It was part of a general change in public opinion. No doubt there are some today who still quietly applaud the killing of hundreds of thousands of Vietnamese civilians in the name of the struggle against Communism and approve, consequently, the head-cracking of protesters against that killing. But once upon a time, the lock-'em-up crowd was a loud majority.

Under the first round of McCarthyism, in the 1950s, well-intentioned liberals who were not rabid anti-Communists or otherwise morally obtuse often managed to find excuses for not defending the targets of the anti-Communist crusade. I have had those people much in mind since 2024, when the United States entered a new McCarthyite phase, with supporters of justice for Palestine serving as the new Communists and identified in the media again as supporters of violence and terror whose presence in American institutions is intolerable. Once again, the institutions of higher education are a hunting ground, and their administrations and boards of trustees are being put to the moral test. As are the leaders of government agencies. These institutions, public as well as private, are themselves in the hunters' sights. Multiple salvos have been fired—protesters arrested on campus, demands made to allow government oversight of teaching and hiring. Government agencies that perform genuinely necessary oversight of matters like water safety and financial fraud have been gutted of their skilled personnel.

The analysts tell us that the groundswell of popular feeling that makes this search-and-destroy mission politically feasible has to do with how people make a living and the inequality with which different ways of doing so have been distributing both prestige and monetary rewards. The point has been made many times: "Democrats are increasingly perceived as the party of college-educated elites, the defenders of a political and economic system that most Americans feel is failing them."[2] Politics in America is increasingly defined by "what could be called a diploma divide."[3] The new McCarthyism thrives when credentialed expertise of any kind can be seen as arrogant, unwarranted privilege.

One premise of this book is that such anti-elitism is not a coherent position. The young Swedish climate activist Greta Thunberg has been described by her critics as privileged, especially perhaps since she started talking about global capitalism as well as climate change and joined a flotilla to break the Gaza blockade. Her followers have been dismissed as "the rich kids of Europe."[4] But are they? In a study of the class composition of environmental activism in 2018 and 2019, two social scientists ask that question and answer it: "Our empirical results challenge the idea that, in

Europe at least, the FFF [Fridays for Future, organized by Greta Thunberg] marches are predominantly populated by 'rich kids.' Rather, despite some cross-national differences, we noted that about half of the surveyed activists self-identified as lower/working or lower-middle classes."[5] Needless to say, those who dismiss the climate activists as rich kids don't always say anything comparable about executives who have made large fortunes in the fossil-fuel industry and don't wait until they're dead to pass their riches on to their own kids. So it's the protesters who are the elite, and these fossil-fuel families aren't. There is something wrong here.

I will be doing a certain amount of low-level sniping like that. I will take sides. (I am in favor of environmental activism.) But this book will also try to take a broader view, at least sometimes. Privilege is not just a hobbyhorse of the anti-elitist right. It is also a favorite theme of the multicultural left.[6] How is that line of argument working out? For a decade or two, initiatives for Diversity, Equity, and Inclusion (DEI) have been summed up in the imperative to "check your privilege!" Some of the backlash against those initiatives, which has not come solely from Trump voters, probably has to do with the sense that there is something misleading in that command, something amiss in the assumption that intolerable privilege must and can be rooted out. Money in the bank is one kind of privilege, but there are so many others. Can they all be rooted out? Would it be a good thing if they could? Racism is intolerable. But maybe there is such a thing as tolerable privilege. The hypothesis seems worth considering.

Privilege needs checking in another sense—as a concept. It needs to be checked on because it is politically discouraging, and unnecessarily so. If racism and sexism are presented as issues of privilege, they become attached to who men and white people *are*, not how they *behave*. Racism and sexism are no longer a matter of things done and said; they are matters of identity. Identity is irrefutable and irreparable. It can't be given up. Presented as matters of privilege rather than as things said and done, racism and sexism invite the guilty-by-birth to indulge in an infinite self-scrutiny, not to say self-flagellation, without any prospect of coming to an end. Self-flagellation has its pleasures, but it allows for no equivalent of economic justice, no purpose like equalizing the distribution of economic resources. Thinking about the privileges of race and gender together with the privileges of wealth and education, and then distinguishing these from each other: This is work that needs doing.

In "Have a Panther to Lunch," published in the *National Review* in February 1970, William F. Buckley reflects on an evening hosted by conductor Leonard Bernstein and his wife Felicia. The purpose of the evening—the *New York Times* Society page would describe it as a "cocktail party," while Bernstein insisted it was just a "meeting"—was to raise money for the legal defense of several members of the Black

Panthers, then awaiting trial in New Haven. Buckley compares the Panthers, tritely, to Nazis. But he ends the piece on a slightly more inventive note. He remarks with pride that, in an hour's conversation with Eldridge Cleaver, he said one thing that made Cleaver truly angry: "The Black Panther Party exists primarily for the satisfaction of white people, rather than black people. The white people like to strut their tolerance."

The ingenious idea that white people "strut their tolerance" reappears in another account of that evening, Tom Wolfe's famous essay "Radical Chic." The essay that coined that influential phrase may be the most famous description of a fundraiser ever written. Funds were indeed raised that evening. The Bernsteins' guests were both well-intentioned and well-heeled; they could afford to contribute. As it happens, the cause to which they were contributing seems to have been a righteous one; the charges against the Panthers were later dropped. In the court of public opinion, however, the defenders of the Panthers lost, and this was largely thanks to the mockery they received from Buckley, Wolfe, and the *New York Times,* whose editorial page referred to the event a day later as "elegant slumming."

Was there ever a chance that the mockery would *not* have worked? Prosperous people, mainly but not entirely white, many of them Jewish (Wolfe makes a big point of their Jewishness), gathering with a small delegation of Black Panthers in a lavishly furnished thirteen-room Upper East Side duplex, with servants (white, as the occasion demanded) handing around platters of upscale hors d'oeuvres—the comedy almost writes itself. Doesn't it?

Comedy aside, another reason for returning to this scene is that the white-people-strutting-their-tolerance line has also returned. *New York Times* columnist David Brooks uses it, for example, in his commentary on the Gaza encampments at Columbia University in the spring of 2024. Brooks, another of Buckley's admirers (Buckley gave him his first job), also wrote the introduction to a 2024 republication of *Radical Chic & Mau-Mauing the Flak Catchers.* What one glimpses here is a shared literary lineage—Buckley, Wolfe, Brooks—that has found considerable success and has done so by reducing other issues, like racism and Gaza, to matters of class resentment.

Brooks is not an outright defender of genocide like his *Times* colleague Bret Stephens. His approach, like Wolfe's, is oblique. He does not say that the people of Gaza, having elected Hamas, deserve to die by the tens of thousands. Rather, he undermines the Gaza protests by calling attention to privilege—the privilege of the Ivy League protesters. The protesters, he insinuates, don't really care about the people of Gaza. What they are doing is scoring status points for themselves, just as Wolfe claims about Bernstein and his circle. They are confirming their identity as a superior caste, an educated and entitled elite.

Wolfe, commenting on Bernstein's withdrawal from the

Black Panther cause in the face of hostile publicity: "Radical Chic, after all, is only radical in style; in its heart it is part of Society and its traditions." Brooks, commenting on how committed Bernstein and his friends really are to the cause of anti-racism: "These people want to care in a way that makes them look gorgeous."

The Columbia protesters in 2024, sleeping for days on the ground, could not reasonably have expected to go around looking gorgeous. Nor, for that matter, is it plausible that they were trying to get arrested, suspended, or expelled, their academic careers terminated or put in jeopardy, their job opportunities canceled, as so many of them have. And yet it must be said that the Buckley-Wolfe-Brooks mode of rhetorical class warfare has done a job on them; as in 1970, it has again proved its value in combat. Brooks all but credits class resentment with the election of Donald Trump, who since his second term began has made a good-faith effort to deport every Gaza protester he can find. Brooks also credits Wolfe with pointing the rhetorical way forward. Wolfe saw, according to Brooks, "that the new coastal elites had made themselves insufferable to working class Americans, and that sooner or later there would be hell to pay." He saw "what the members of the beau monde were too oblivious to see. That if you told the people in Queens or Topeka that the rich white people of the Upper East Side were throwing parties for the Panthers, they would fall all over themselves laughing."

Was it possible, *is* it possible, for this mode of rhetorical class warfare to fail, or be seen through? Was there, *is* there any reason why ordinary people in Queens or Topeka might *not* fall all over themselves laughing at social-justice fundraisers or protests held by people who are not themselves being shot or bombed or starved? Much depends on how we understand words like elite, privilege, and entitlement, how we answer questions like who or what is responsible for economic inequality. That's the agenda here.

Wolfe reports with relish on the sumptuousness of the Bernstein apartment: "the moldings, the sconces, the Roquefort morsels rolled in crushed nuts, the servants, the elevator attendant and the doorman downstairs in their white dickeys, the marble lobby, the brass struts on the marquee out front." You get the point: The Panthers are living every day in the face of violent death at the hands of the police, and they are threatening to answer violence with violence; how unaccustomed to such very serene, very expensive things they must be! But you may also ask yourself: How accustomed to these very serene, very expensive things are the ordinary people of Queens or Topeka? Tom Wolfe, for his part, is clearly *very* accustomed to them. Otherwise, he could hardly name them with such quiet authority. Personally, not that my own class background is relevant, I would have trouble telling sconces from dickeys, let alone identifying "aged and seasoned marble" or "fruitwood," "teapoys" or "japanned chairs." If I could imagine myself as Joe Public—I probably have as good a claim as Wolfe—I wouldn't be confident that Wolfe is speaking for the likes of me.

Wolfe writes:

> One's heart does cry out—quite spontaneously!—upon hearing how the police have dealt with the Panthers . . . well, anyway, one truly feels for them. On the other hand—on the second track in one's mind, that is—one also has a sincere concern for maintaining a proper East Side life-style in New York Society . . . For example, one *must* have a weekend place, in the country or by the shore, all year round preferably, but certainly from the middle of May to the middle of September. It is hard to get across to outsiders an understanding of how *absolute* such apparently trivial needs are. One feels them in one's solar plexus.

Here Wolfe is ventriloquizing the rich and clueless. We are supposed to think that this performance is satirical. But having lent his voice to others, he has trouble getting that voice back, convincing us that his own voice is different from theirs. He can't help but sound like he knows a lot about this lifestyle, and from the inside.

If so, Wolfe must have some other beef with the partygoers. It turns out he does. To him, they represent *new* money. You can tell when he uses the word "parvenu" (one of the essay's many French expressions) and when he sneers at the "horde of rank climbers." Going back in history, he places the social ascension of the Bernsteins and their friends in a sequence of other "new-money upheavals." The premise seems to be that Wolfe has the right to look down at new money because, in his heart of hearts, he identifies not with the people in Queens or Topeka, but with *old* money. That would go with the trademark white linen three-piece suits, a Southern gentleman's invitation to *Vogue*, name-checked in the piece, to ask him for an interview. The contempt of old money for new money may give the people of Queens and Topeka a momentary thrill, since it splashes some mud on the partygoing clothes of the powerful. But pleasures of that sort wear off pretty quickly. You would have to ask yourself: Did the old money think more respectfully about their less-opulent neighbors than today's rich do? And you would have to respond: Probably not.

One big difference between old money and new money, in Wolfe's view, is that the new money is insecure—he begins and ends his essay with one of Bernstein's vivid anxiety dreams—and, in its insecurity, has something to prove. A second big difference, which is also an explanation for the first, is that what is called new money may not *be* money—that is, may owe its social position to something other than money. Brooks writes: "Wolfe read Max Weber at Yale and it all clicked: Life is a contest for status. Some people think humans are driven by money, or love, or to heal the wounds they suffered in childhood, but Wolfe put the relentless scramble up the pecking order at the center of his worldview." Stop and think about this for a minute. You can be driven by a contest for status, *or* you can be driven by money. Brooks says here, plain as day, that the drive to obtain status is not the same as the drive to obtain money. Prestige is a different animal, a separate and not necessarily convertible currency. This is an idea that is indeed associated with the great sociologist Max Weber, about whom I will be saying more below. But in that case, there is something misleading and even perverse about Wolfe's relentless attention to the trappings of wealth.

Brooks tries to explain all this in his introduction to the 2024 reprint: "The members of the new cultural elite could never be so secure. Their status—their very reason for being—was based on their own superior sensibility." Please pardon a bit of close reading: Isn't this ambiguous? Is Brooks saying here that they *feel* superior (in which case, shame on them), or on the contrary that they *have* a superior sensibility for which they have been legitimately rewarded? He doesn't pursue the second possibility, but "based on" means it's there, and it's intriguingly at variance with what Brooks seems to want to be saying. Let me put this another way. Brooks writes that this "rising elite" is made up of the ethnically diverse group of "formerly unthinkables—Catholics, Jews, Black people," who in Wolfe's view were displacing "the old blue blood Protestant elite—the Astors, the Whitneys, the Rockefellers." Unlike the old, the new elite did not owe its position to bloodlines and the inherited ownership of land or to huge fortunes amassed in industry by fair means or foul, more likely foul. No, they owed their ascension to work in "culture and the media." Work in culture and the media is dramatically different from how the Astors, Whitneys, and Rockefellers accumulated their fortunes. (Look them up—the picture is not pretty.) Work in culture and the media also does not imply the accumulation of wealth on anything like the same scale. Unlike the possessors of the old money, these new moneyed elites might not have ample and diversified portfolios to fall back on. No doubt people like Bernstein (composer and conductor) and Barbara Walters (guest and national news anchor) earned higher than average salaries. But their eminence is essentially social, not financial. It is entirely founded, as Brooks admits, on recognition of their cultural achievement. Recognition of achievement is always genuinely precarious; it generates inescapable insecurity. In Brooks's own account, this is an elite based on prestige in people's eyes, not on money in the bank.

Wolfe's takedown of the Bernsteins' evening with the Panthers, then, is strangely not about the money after all. Indeed, you could almost say his satire of the new elite takes attention *away* from the power of money, which has arguably never loosened its commanding grip on how we all live. It's unclear that elite is even the right word for them. Or that the people of Queens and Topeka have reason to find them as amusing as Wolfe and Brooks do. If there is a class story here, it's a story whose basis lies closer to the experience of what Americans call the middle class.

For white or Jewish or middle-class or culture-and-media people, how does strutting their tolerance supposedly become a means of rising in the world, or earning a better-than-average living? The hypothesis seems implausible, but Brooks takes a shot at explaining it. His explanation is that they are engaging in what amounts to demagoguery: "rising to the social stratosphere by ostentatiously demonstrating their solidarity with the oppressed, securing their place atop the structures of power by striking radical poses, and pretending to support tearing those structures down." But this makes no sense. Why would it work? If the people addressed by this demagoguery are falling all over themselves with laughter, why would they be taken in by anyone striking radical poses? How could this strategy have any chance of succeeding? Why should we believe that it even is a strategy? What Brooks, like Wolfe and Buckley, will never question is the assumption that when white people or middle-class people engage in some sort of protest, they must be trying to serve their own collective self-interest. The right-wing rhetoricians don't need to say it, so deep is their belief: Political position-taking always favors the particular material interests of the group to which one belongs.[7] Says who?

According to sociologist Frank Parkin, middle-class radicalism may not look like radicalism at all, at least to some people, and the reason is that it doesn't fit this model. In the chapter "Radical Politics and Social Class," Parkin brings up movements against apartheid and capital punishment as well as the movement for nuclear disarmament, the main subject of his book. He argues that "these goals are intrinsically different from those pursued by working-class movements in that they offer no particular benefits to those who support them—such benefits are felt to accrue to others (e.g. Negroes, political prisoners) or to society as a whole rather than to themselves specifically."[8] This is no doubt oversimplified, in part because there has always been a strong element of working-class support for universal goals. It is also problematic because "material," Parkin's term for working-class goals, would certainly apply to, say, preventing the use of nuclear weapons or stopping the appalling flow of fatalities in a conventional war, like Vietnam. Not dying is a material goal. So is slowing down the rate of climate change. Saying no to a government-caused famine does not satisfy my own hunger, but it's certainly not immaterial.

In "Have a Panther to Lunch," Buckley expresses the wish that the Bernstein event should have been televised "so that the hungry of the world, like you and me," could have observed it. *Like you and me*? That is, as the saying goes, rich. Buckley has conceded to critics who were understandably impatient with his memoir that he simply did not know what it was like, living the life he was born into, to be without the services of servants, maids, and chauffeurs. Even if he's trying to be funny with "like you and me," as he may be, it's probably a mistake to identify himself with the hungry of the world. In a time when the people of Gaza have been deliberately starved for months by Israeli government policy and as I write are still being starved, with many dying every day, it would be obscene for people who get their three square meals a day to identify themselves with the Gazans. But it would not be a mistake to protest, loud and clear and without coming up for air, against how Gaza is being treated. Those of us who are not hungry have that right. Anti-elitism should not be allowed to stand in our way.

WHO'S ALLOWED TO PROTEST?

ONE

WHAT DO ELITES LIVE ON?

What did the French Romantic writer Gérard de Nerval live on? The question is posed by an obscure seventy-five-year-old volume entitled *De Quoi Vivait Gérard de Nerval* that popped up in a footnote[1] and that the Columbia University library took several days to deliver from somewhere off-site. The book, written by one Clément Borgal, previously unknown to me, begins with the writer's death on a winter street in Paris in 1855, followed by testimony from Nerval's friends that lack of funds was not to blame for it. Nerval's body was found without a coat, and in his trouser pockets only some small change. Did his poverty lead to his suicide? Was this a classic case of the starving bohemian writer, a proto-*luftmensch* living on nothing but air until he couldn't bear that life any longer?

In the end, Borgal's book decides that, however one tries to explain his suicide (he had suffered more than once from mental illness), Nerval did not die of poverty. His destitution was not a self-sacrificial gesture meant, as the French put it, to dumbfound (*épater*) the bourgeois. We should not believe Nerval's friend Théophile Gautier, who said that if Nerval was not rich, it was only because "he didn't want to be and disdained to be."[2] Nerval had been the recipient of a not inconsiderable inheritance. He lived the high life on that inheritance until it was gone, and he kept living much the same life afterward.[3] To judge from his correspondence, especially his letters to his father, he was never not in pursuit of a stable, secure income. He could always sell his books, though not for very much. His newspaper articles were a more reliable source of revenue. But his earnings didn't keep up with his taste for foreign travel, which he also used as material for his writing, and other expensive pleasures. The day before his death, he gave a coin to a friend's servant, who didn't ask for or need it. Without his performative self-indulgence, which included walking a pet lobster on a leash, he could have managed well enough.

Why is the question of Nerval's livelihood worth revisiting? Because, for one thing, managing well enough has suddenly become visible as a category that, although it seems commonsensical, lacks a place of its own in arguments about economic inequality, arguments which these days seem unavoidable. For Nerval, an artist who also had at least intermittent political commitments, and for the many like him, there need to be safe landing spots between the polemical extremes of lethal indigence and opulent privilege. Perhaps the real issue for him, as for any *luftmensch*, is not how good a living he made—he had to pawn his coat, but he also followed daily prices on the Paris stock exchange—but that society should be willing to pay him *anything at all*, given that his goal was, at least to some extent, the criticism of society.

How Nerval made a living is also a live question because the Parisian bohemia to which Nerval belonged is the crucial case study in the sociologist Pierre Bourdieu's *The Rules of Art: Genesis and Structure of the Literary Field*. In the twenty-first century, protest and countercultural activity continue to be described as bohemian, and the sociological theory of modern art Bourdieu developed in his bohemia book remains both influential and intriguingly unsettled.[4] How enthusiastic was Bourdieu about bohemian poverty? *Was* it in fact poverty? Was Nerval "elegantly slumming" in bohemia? It's hard to tell.

In rough outline, Bourdieu's theory is this: Bohemian artists in the nineteenth century discovered that, in art, you could succeed by failing. The less your art sold or (even better) the more you were seen to be spurning the conventional, salable values of the artistic marketplace, the higher your prestige could rise in the parallel field of aesthetic judgment and the more "symbolic capital" (Bourdieu's phrase) you could accumulate within that field. When you refused to play the game, you were still playing to win. Pushed far enough, this logic would suggest that Nerval's death in poverty was a kind of victory against the marketplace, and a victory from which writers and artists since then have benefited. It's also possible that, though this didn't work for

Nerval, the status won was ultimately convertible into cash. Bourdieu presents the logic without coming down one way or the other on the convertibility question.

According to this logic, art for art's sake is really a disguised competition for status. In Bourdieu's eyes, so is most everything else. As a picture of social life in general, status competition—the desire to look, feel, or be superior to other people—is a little unbalanced. It's a very real thing, of course; it would be ridiculous to wish away that side of human nature. But isn't it only one side? Imagined as a universal key to human conduct, especially the most righteous sorts, the status-competition model has arguably gotten out of hand. Recently, for example, it has been put to work discrediting not just practice in art, but protest in politics. All these protesters want, like the bohemian artist of Nerval's time, is to make themselves look good, we are told, or to look better than everyone else.

When I hear statements like that, the philosophical concept that comes to mind is cynicism. Cynicism has a long and respectable history; some have always found it an attractive way of looking at the world, and it is arguably more attractive today than it has ever been. Both German philosopher Peter Sloterdijk and British literary critic Helen Small link cynicism's power in the present to Nietzsche's idea that, if we are honest, we will admit that our actions are self-interested, especially actions that might seem piously altruistic. Sloterdijk argues that to the cynic, "the force of circumstances" justifies "the instinct for self-preservation." Aren't we all glad of any excuse, like the force of circumstance, that permits us to prioritize our self-preservation? Self-preservation is what we wanted to prioritize anyway. Small, opposing Nietzsche directly, writes, "The identification of 'self-interest' as 'an individual's basic motive' is too quick and too sweeping: a basic egoism can account for some of our motives, but not all."[5] True enough, but Nietzsche's mistake is encouraged by our capitalist society's embrace of the underlying principle: The pursuit of self-interest guarantees individual freedom and eventually benefits everyone.

In any case, cynics think they are smarter than other people, and maybe they are. If you look at the world through Bourdieu's lens, suspicious of anything that smacks of disinterestedness, you are less likely to be taken for a sucker. Like the ideology of the free market, cynicism suggests that politics, a collective activity, would be a waste of energy for you. If the same logic that applies to artistic disinterestedness also applies to political commitment, and readers of Bourdieu are not the only ones who take the logic in this direction, it follows that claims to be speaking for the common good or the good of others are as shady as claims to be creating art for art's sake. Knowing that any motives not aimed at your own profit will be open to mockery is not an incentive to speak idealistically, let alone altruistically. Someone who suspects they are surrounded by cynics is less likely to sound off in an empathetic way about this or that category of victims, and the people standing around them may be grateful that they hold their tongue. Cynicism's power to make your friends curb their enthusiasm, politically speaking, must count, for many, as one of its virtues.[6]

Nerval was not a cynic. Living as he did in the heady run-up to the 1848 revolutions, he declared himself a republican and was described as something of a socialist. He was fascinated by the utopian thinker Restif de la Bretonne, who is credited with the first use of the word communist (he's also credited with the naming of shoe fetishism, *rétifisme*). He imagined a society that would have no need of money. His admirer Nerval was briefly imprisoned for his part in student demonstrations. Student demonstrations since October 2023 are another reason for reaching back to Bourdieu's analysis of Nerval's circle. Bourdieu doubts that the artists of Paris's nineteenth-century bohemia were really disinterested. As we have seen, the same doubts have been directed at the student protesters of 2024. One thing that irritated certain observers about the Gaza encampments was their display of concern for people far away. These observers, in some cases encouraged by the reading of Bourdieu, preferred to understand the protests as the concealed pursuit of student self-interest.

Many were probably hearkening back to the Vietnam War protests of the 1960s. In their own time, the anti-war protests were often psychologized, and therefore politically trivialized, as expressing the Oedipal rebellion of children against their parents. Steven Kelman's 1970 memoir, *Push Comes to Shove: The Escalation of Student Protest*, speaks of the protesters' "psychological self-interest."[7] Standard, not unsympathetic interpretations of the sixties movements refer to the students' desire both to break from their parents and to find a heroic equivalent to what the parents' generation had suffered in the Depression and World War II. Paul Berman writes: "The young people wanted to redeem their lost souls. They wanted to leave behind the privileges and comforts of middle-class student life and go fight in the street the way the heroes of the Resistance had gone into the street to fight against the Nazis."[8] These sentences are respectful enough, but the rebel-without-a-cause trope, which imagines students seeking a political purpose in order to fill some nameless emptiness in their privileged lives, seeking above all to satisfy their own *need* for meaning or redemption, implies, again, that the students of 1968 were fundamentally self-interested.

It is a truism about the Vietnam-era protests that they were motivated in part by the threat of conscription, the prospect of being sent off to kill or be killed, and in this sense were indeed self-interested. The threat did not target all classes equally. While enrolled, students had the advantage over nonstudents of being able to "defer" being drafted. Then the deferments were canceled. And then the draft itself was canceled, at the end of 1972 the U.S. Army became all-volunteer, and the protests petered out. Of course, self-interest was a factor. But whether or not this understanding of the Vietnam protests is convincing (American involvement in the war was also petering out), comparing the protests of the two eras on a scale of self-interest and disinterestedness would seem to favor, morally speaking, the more recent protesters.[9] As with Vietnam, the Gaza encampments were protests against American involvement in bodily harm inflicted on people at a considerable distance. But the Gaza protests happened in a period when there was no draft and thus no threat of bodily harm to American protesters except, as it turned out, from campus security and the police. Both cynics and zealous supporters of the Israeli military, who were sometimes the same people, found this appearance of moral generosity galling.[10] In the absence of conscription, they had to cast about for a theory that would highlight the protesters' self-interest and draw the protest into disrepute. In the case of David Brooks, cynicism fastened itself to their privilege. The protesters, he argued, were only trying to shore up their privileged status as an elite.

Writing in the 1990s, Brooks had already used Bourdieu's signature analysis as the key to the class he called bobos, for bourgeois bohemians. In *Bobos in Paradise: The New Upper Class and How They Got There*, he announces: "Those who most vociferously and publicly renounce material success win prestige and honor that can be converted into lucre."[11]

Countercultural prestige can be converted into legal tender. This conversion is also a parable of what happens, as Brooks tells the story, when the radicalism of the sixties movements happily allows itself to be co-opted into the commercialism of the "greed is good" 1980s, becoming a source of profitable coolness and cultural creativity.

In his commentary on our own era, Brooks brings back the idea that supposed radicalism is always complicit with the for-profit system and therefore doesn't have to be taken seriously. But this time he attaches the idea to what has become a mainstream talking point: anti-elitism. In the culture wars of the sixties and seventies, the political right *defended* elitism, which it saw the egalitarian radicals as attacking. See for example William A. Henry III's volume *In Defense of Elitism*, which takes on the radicals' "misguided egalitarianism."[12] Today, of course, the right is *attacking* elitism. The big news of our time is that the issue of class hierarchy, borrowed from the left, has turned into a battering ram for the right. Sociology has played a part in this reversal.

The right seems to have decided that Bourdieu, man of the left, scourge of the elites, and the top sociologist of his generation, can help remove student radicals from their perch on the moral high ground while adding a sheen of academic respectability to mainstream opinion-makers who are already toeing the government line. In short, they have decided that Bourdieu is on their side. In a *New York*

Times editorial in June 2024 entitled "The Sins of the Educated Class," published just after the Gaza encampments, Brooks quotes the sociologist Musa al-Gharbi's *We Have Never Been Woke*.[13] Citing Bourdieu, just as Brooks himself did, al-Gharbi disparages student demonstrators at Columbia University on the grounds that they chose to go to Columbia in the first place only because of a "desire to be more elite than other college graduates."

Elitism is also the clincher for Brooks. If you want to know the meaning of the 2024 protests, all you need to know, he suggests, is that they happened "mostly at elite colleges." If this were a debate, I would object that Brooks is using the hoariest of rhetorical fallacies, poisoning the well: You insinuate that your opponents can't be trusted (they are elites!) without having to engage with the issues they have raised. For Brooks, it goes without saying that the protests have nothing to do with what the protestors say they are about: the bombing of a densely populated area and the massive civilian deaths that have resulted. This poisoning of the well has long been standard operating procedure at the *New York Times*. When the *Times* and other mainstream media covered the protests at Columbia in 1968, Todd Gitlin writes in *The Sixties*, they "cast a blind eye on Columbia's owning slums, cooperating with the military, disdaining students; apparently it agreed with the radicals that 'the issue is not the issue.'"[14]

For Brooks and the *Times*, as for Bourdieu's sociology, the issue is *never* the issue. The protests must be understood instead as an event within a particular social group, namely the elite. And the elite, Brooks says, has shifted to the left. The non-elite know better than to protest over such things as the bombing of Gaza; the poor of America, students or not, have other concerns on their minds, as well they should.[15] After all, Brooks implies, what are the people of Gaza to them? Why should they care about these faraway Arabs? What they care about is their own jobs. But wait—that's the same as the elites! The elites, too, care first and foremost about their jobs. But the jobs they care about are harder to get, more desirable. An overproduction of educated elites (the fault of elite institutions!) has led to elite underemployment. As a result, there are now "ferocious power struggles with other elites." The upshot: Social protest makes sense when it is considered as a weapon in those struggles. Like the refusal of bohemian artists to sell their art, student protests against the massacre in Gaza are "quintessential luxury beliefs." By circulating luxury beliefs, or holier-than-thou principles, you display your higher status, or advance a claim that you *deserve* higher status, hence that you deserve a better job. Political position-taking is just political posturing, making moves in "a struggle for social position." Brooks concludes that demonstrations do nothing to rescue those in whose name the demonstrations are organized. Al-Gharbi agrees, arguing that the demonstrators never cared about the people of Gaza in the first place. They were only concerned with themselves.

Let us pause briefly here, in the interests of common decency, to recall that *no one* managed to rescue the Palestinians of Gaza, who are still dying of starvation and military violence as I write. Few even made the slightest effort. Certainly not Brooks or al-Gharbi. Many Americans saw the mangled corpses of Palestinian women and children on their screens and knew that they represented thousands more. They may well have flinched, knowing also that the US government was actively supporting the bombing. And then they said and did nothing to discourage further slaughter or hold the politicians accountable. The student activists, on the other hand, were doing what they could, however little it may have been. If only for the purpose of argument, it would be satisfying to exhibit the "Thank you, Columbia!" banner that Gazans composed, photographed, and disseminated when the Columbia encampments went up. If the Palestinians who advertised their gratitude in this way in 2024 are still alive after the total destruction of their neighborhoods and the deaths of so many of their neighbors, their opinions on the argument of Brooks and al-Gharbi would seem worth trying to ascertain.

Watching real-time videos of the corpses pulled from the rubble of apartment buildings and knowing that this bombing is being supported by your government and by the corporations in which your university's endowment is invested, hence also by your university, led by its trustees, some of those trustees themselves invested in and even helping direct those corporations, like the arms manufacturer Lockheed Martin, which supplies the Israel Defense Forces—these are motives for protest that ought to speak for themselves. Why the sociologists feel obliged to look elsewhere for the protesters' true motives is a bit of a puzzle. Enough of a puzzle, perhaps, so that one may risk some mean-spiritedness and inquire into the sociologists' own motives. When al-Gharbi says that student protesters enrolled at Columbia University in order to increase their elite status, he's begging to be asked in his turn why he himself, having chosen to do his own PhD at Columbia, would not deserve to have his motives impugned on the same grounds.[16] When al-Gharbi says that the protesters cared only about themselves, a psychologist could invoke the concept of projection. Is there a thought he's had about himself that makes al-Gharbi uncomfortable, and that he therefore pushes off onto others of whom he can then disapprove? When he invokes a worldview that has no room for motives that aren't slimy, can he avoid the idea that, to others, his own motives will look equally slimy?

Slimy or not, that worldview is logically inconsequential. If status seeking is the motive for everything and everyone, as al-Gharbi seems to assume, then it's as if it were true for nobody. Raising the point has no moral consequences. It's a waste of time.

But okay, if the sociologists have put the examination of motives on the agenda, let us overcome our own polite reticence and burrow a little deeper into theirs. In the first sentence of his book, al-Gharbi tells the reader: "Until 2016, I'd spent virtually my entire life in a smallish southern Arizona military town . . ." Why is the information about the small military town in Arizona relevant? Well, moving from his book to his personal website, one finds the beginnings of an answer. His relations with the US military are deeper than geography: "I'm from a military family going back generations. My maternal grandfather fought in WWII, Korea and Vietnam. My father helped coordinate NATO operations during operation Desert Storm. My mother and my stepdad were both in the army too—alongside many of my siblings and cousins. I was raised in the community surrounding the U.S. Army's principal intelligence base." It does not require an advanced degree in sociology to look at this biographical detail and speculate about the effect this background might have had on the author's views of anti-war protesters. Being raised in a military town and by a family that has earned its living in military employment for generations makes some sense of the fact that, in al-Gharbi's listing of the "genuinely marginalized and disadvantaged" about whom the student protesters supposedly don't really care, no provision is made for caring about the killed and maimed victims of American military violence. The wars in Afghanistan and Iraq, like Palestine, get no mention in the book's index. The casual reader is left wondering how al-Gharbi explains, in the absence of a draft, the massive protests against those wars, like the record-setting protests of February 15, 2003, against the imminent US invasion of Iraq. Those anti-war protests were not merely American. They were happening worldwide. What could have made all those people so indignant about the violence meted out by the US military, al-Gharbi's family business, the source of his family's income?

One of the strange things about the privilege argument (it's really a thinly disguised sneer) is its gravitational attraction to anti-war protest. It's as if privilege, elitism, and class were rhetorical weapons that would ordinarily be kept under lock and key out of fear that they might go off in the presence of, say, issues involving working hours or salaries or health insurance, where the consequences might be politically inconvenient to the wielders. It's as if privilege, elitism, and class could only be taken out of the gun locker when the subject on the floor was militarism—that is, to defend patriotic bloodshed. Anti-war protest may or may not be characteristically middle-class; the question is worth asking. But it's also worth asking whether finger-pointing at social inequality has a special mission to undermine the credibility of militarism's critics. That would say something about its own credibility.

Those of us who cannot stop thinking about economic inequality—I myself have sounded off about it a lot—have a responsibility to consider how much the persistence of inequality may have to do with the persistence of militarism. We know militarism is bad for democracy. Maybe it's also bad for economic equality? It's not just the huge amount of government spending that goes to defense and the effect the national-security framework has on the rights of workers in those industries, or the dependence of welfare, as a strategy to protect capitalism from itself, on warfare, which is to say the dependence of capitalism itself on warfare. In his book *Men of Ideas: A Sociologist's View,* Lewis Coser discusses the tendency of intellectuals to define themselves by the taking of political positions. Historically, many of the positions taken by intellectuals have been denunciations of inequality. In the five years between the hardback edition of Coser's book (1965) and the paperback edition (1970), Coser sees an enormous change in the self-defining positions taken by intellectuals. The change, he says, is the result of the Vietnam War. What has intervened in those five years is, in his words, "one of the most profound watersheds in the history of American intellectuals."[17] He is not 100 percent enthusiastic about student-led protest against the Vietnam War, but he is almost stupefied by its tremendous scale and intensity. "The movement of protest against American involvement in Vietnam has assumed proportions unprecedented not only in America, but in fact in all of modern Western history. It probably surpasses in intellectual consequence both the abolitionist movement and the French Dreyfusard campaign, and it certainly surpasses them in numerical size." In retrospect, this looks like it might be an excited overstatement.[18] But it raises the question of whether there is a special place for war in the explanation of middle-class radicalism—of whether indignation at mass killing, or at the mass killing of noncombatants, or at the mass killing of noncombatants in one's own name, is so viscerally powerful that it rivals economic deprivation and self-interest as a reason for protest.

You may be quite clear as to what side you're on about the Gaza protesters. Or you may not. But wherever you stand, there are holes to be filled, confusions to be cleared up. It needs to be said, for example, that Brooks's anti-elitism has a certain plausibility to the very people he's accusing. The Gaza protesters at elite schools were often the first to bring up the uncomfortable subject of their unearned advantages. Privilege is something of which they frequently accused themselves. They were obviously not trying to say that their protests should therefore be ignored. Does common sense have any reassurance to offer them? There are perhaps some things that they and future protesters would do well to hear, if only we could figure out what those things are.

Today, anti-elitism nurtures two of the Republican Party's most cherished projects: its attacks on higher education and its dismantling of federal agencies. Both the universities and the agencies of the federal government stand accused of being staffed by experts who think they know better than ordinary people and, in their arrogance, use their power to propagate woke ideology. As mentioned above, Brooks's "The Sins of the Educated Class" ends with a menacing prophecy of Donald Trump's victory in November 2024, a victory that would be achieved, Brooks warned, with significant working-class support and would be followed by a massive attack on the institutions of higher education. This has come to pass. The last sentence of the piece is "The lesson for those of us in the educated class is to seriously reform the system we have created or be prepared to be run over." As I write, higher education *is* being run over. The "reforms" the Trump administration has called for higher education to carry out, like handing over potentially incriminating information about student protesters for the purpose of arresting and possibly deporting them and allowing the government to take control over matters of teaching and hiring, could not pass muster with anyone who believes in the independent mission of higher education. But not everyone does. I add that there are other reforms of higher education of which the same could not be said and that might possibly make a dent in Trump's working-class support.

If Bourdieu's status-conscious cynicism about elites has been getting so much play, and on the right as well as the left, it seems like a good time to stop and ask: What *is* an elite? Sometimes the word seems to indicate only people who are very good at what they do, like an elite team of firefighters. One might say that if there are such things as unearned privileges, then there are also earned ones; an elite team of firefighters has earned its privileges, such as they are. As have air traffic controllers and financial fraud regulators and many other kinds of specialized workers that society depends on. Bourdieu himself seems less than transparent on this question. Does he think elites, unlike most firefighters, are rich? When he and his followers use the word elite, are they referring to what some of us used to call the ruling class? Is that the implication when student protesters are described as privileged—that these students belong to the group of our society's ultimate decision-makers? Do they belong, say, with William F. Buckley, who, when readers rolled their eyes at his autobiography, explained, "It simply happens to be the case that I have never in my entire life been without servants, maids, and chauffeurs"?[19] And supposing that student protesters *are* privileged, in this or some lesser sense of the word, would it follow that their protests don't have to be taken seriously? Can we assume that radicalism emerging from, say, the middle class—the large swathe of people who are neither rich nor starving—should be ignored as egocentric, ephemeral, or insincere, even when what it's protesting is, say, military violence?

Before he remade himself at the end of his life as another petition-signing, position-declaiming public intellectual, Bourdieu took every opportunity to affirm that his work was done within and for the field of sociology. His sociological writing was intended, among other things, to further sociology's interests.[20] He was assuming, correctly, that as a discipline in competition with other disciplines, sociology *has* interests. From the outset it has struggled to defend the distinctness of its disciplinary object—society—against, for example, the scholarly imperialism of its powerful neighbor economics, whose disciplinary object, roughly speaking, is money.[21] Economists might ask: Who needs the concept of society to explain anything? They might feel that money, or the desire to maximize one's wealth, explains the same phenomena that sociology tries to explain, and explains them better. It was partly in order to claim a distinct area of jurisdiction for itself that sociology, as a fledgling discipline, made one of its founding gestures: separating social status from the possession of money—in other words, from class. Class has a tendency to generate two politically polarized sides. Status doesn't. Status tends to generate a potentially infinite number of subtle gradations. In this or that case, sociology was eager to show, you could have high status in society without being rich. By this gesture, it gave itself jurisdiction over a distinct object that could not be better explained, say, by reference to class or wealth. Separating status from wealth or class, as Max Weber did, is of course what is accomplished again in today's renewed culture wars by the targeting of status-conscious elites, a targeting which may not be cynical in its tone but is cynical in its substance. You have heard the refrain before: Whatever they may say, elites are only looking out for themselves. "This struggle is not waged on behalf of others": These words, from *The Origins of Postcommunist Elites: From Prague Spring to the Breakup of Czechoslovakia* by the sociologist Gil Eyal, crystallize the influence of Bourdieu on the conceptualization of elites as invariably self-interested but, in their claims to represent others, reluctant to admit it.[22]

David Brooks describes his method, which involves mocking the comforts and privileges of student activists and other bourgeois bohemians, as "comic sociology." Given sociology's founding logic, it should not be surprising that today's sociology-inflected discourse of elites, comic or not, is somewhat forgetful about the realities of money. This forgetfulness begs to be corrected. Let us, then, take a few stops along that well-traveled path. Let us try to follow the money.

Following the money is not as straightforward a procedure as it might seem. Philosophically considered, the rough premise should be that there is no such thing as clean money. I'll spare you examples of the steps—probably not many—that would lead back in any given case from the amassing of supposedly clean money to the eventual source of that money in the dirt of an unjust social system.[23] Dirty money, yes. Clean money, no. In other words, let's say that all money is dirty. But some money is less dirty than other money. It would seem to follow, therefore, that some money-following methodology must exist that would avoid too much moralizing. As a small step in that direction, we might assume, for starters, that to achieve artistic status without putting aside any money at all is not a viable moral option. Absolute failure to convert your prestige into money might leave you to hang yourself on a freezing Paris street, like Nerval. No one can live on air.[24] Let's begin by setting the bar low. The desire not to starve ought to be morally uncontroversial.

Evidence of gross and increasing economic inequality in America is easily available and has been for years. The facts and figures are well-known, and yet they are probably still shocking, as they deserve to be. Repeating them here is unnecessary. Given how much worldly evil has been caused by the pursuit of financial self-interest by the managers of hedge funds and private equity funds and billionaires helping elect corrupt, self-dealing politicians, following the money begets the expectation that what will follow can only be an exposé. I have great respect for the exposé genre, but that genre can't do all the work if you begin by distinguishing, as I do, between having *a lot* of money and merely having *some* money—say, enough to live on, or even a bit more than that, enough to feel that you are not one illness or car crash away from financial disaster. That distinction may also seem uncontroversial, but keeping it in mind will help clear away some of the confusion that surrounds words like privilege and elite, words which arguably (so I will argue) get in the way of actual efforts to achieve more equality. Some elites are firefighters. Not all privilege is intolerable.

Paradoxical as it may seem, the main effect of finger-pointing at elites is often to divert attention away from money and from the rich and powerful who benefit most from our political system and have the most control over it. Doug Henwood, one of the few leftist thinkers to examine in serious detail what the left still calls the ruling class, rejects "conceptions of a ruling class that center on PC-obsessed, organic food-eating urban elites." He goes on, "That set has some influence, especially among the liberal wing of the consciousness industry, but it doesn't shape the political economy." It's the shaping of the political economy, he argues, that ought to be decisive in defining who does and doesn't belong to the ruling class: "The ruling class consists of a politically engaged capitalist class, operating through lobbying groups. Financial support for politicians, think tanks, and publicity, that meshes with a senior political class that directs the machinery of the state."[25] To put this another way: The characteristic members of the ruling class are not skilled, educated, credentialed professionals like lawyers, doctors, and consultants. The ruling class is made up of the owners of the firms for which those skilled professionals work. Henwood argues, therefore, against lambasting the "privilege" (he puts the word privilege in quotation marks) of so-called elites. They do not belong to the ruling class as he defines it. Indeed, they may be capable of serving as oppositional thinkers and activists, people ready to cast a cold eye on that ruling class and encourage those who want to do away with it and the economic inequality it depends on: "Growing up bourgeois confers some advantages—time to study, as well as exposure to the nature of power—often denied to people further down the social hierarchy." It does the cause of equality no good, he implies, if these advantages are treated as incriminating evidence of a privilege that no one should enjoy rather than as signifiers of a well-being that one day will hopefully be available to any and all.[26]

If "privileged" is understood as applicable to anyone who is not desperately needy, the word is leading us astray. It encourages us to measure economic inequality by the wrong yardstick. That is the implicit premise of the Urban Institute's 2024 report on "The True Cost of Economic Security." Rather than testifying to "acute need," the report casts a broader net, looking for those who may be "just getting by" but are not "economically secure."[27] Economic security stands for what it takes to live sustainably, or, as the report puts it, to thrive. Madeline Leung Coleman underlines the report's findings for New York City: "Over 60% of New Yorkers do not meet the threshold. Of families with children, it's 72%."[28] These figures are more significant than the usual poverty statistics because they take in more of the daily struggle of a large proportion of American households. But they matter for another reason, more relevant here: because they recognize economic security as something other than privilege—that is, as a morally defensible goal. In other words, they recognize the positive value of having *some* rather than *a lot* of money. Let us describe this criterion as a quantity of income and savings (more than half of all Americans have no retirement savings at all) that could be mentioned in neighborly gossip without embarrassment. Or as managing well enough.

Embarrassment is probably the first reaction to anyone asking what you, or anyone else, lives on. The question posed by Nerval's existence leads into a minefield that most people have instinctively learned to avoid. There are unwritten rules against asking. There even appear to be unwritten rules about people, unasked, *telling* you what they live on, or how much they make, as Edmund Wilson does in *The Cold War and the Income Tax* and as Walter Benn Michaels does in *The Trouble with Diversity*. When they choose to divulge, are they implying that they need have no shame because they deserve what they get? Or are they implying on the contrary that shame is unnecessary and misplaced because money is not a good measure of what *anyone* deserves? Is there egalitarian dissent lurking behind the naming of amounts? Or does it depend on the amounts? ($175,000 per year for Michaels, an academic, writing in 2006.) It would be useful to begin shining some light into that murkiness.[29]

The moral and political perplexity that surrounds sources of income can be illustrated by a brief discussion of the exotic word rentier. What is a rentier? Often it is a landlord, someone who takes in rent from property they own. Often it is not an individual landlord but a corporation that owns a lot of real estate and takes in rent from lots of people.[30] And often the property that produces the rent is not real estate but other investments, like stocks and bonds, and the form the rent takes is interest, dividends, and capital gains. A more restricted definition of the rentier makes the return on accumulated wealth, perhaps wealth accumulated by a parent or grandparent, into a larger proportion of the rentier's total income and thus also a decisive fact about their selfhood. In that case, the rentier becomes someone who "lives on" income from property or investments, whether or not they also work—a rentier does not live on air. In other words, they are someone who does *not* depend on income from the work that they may also perform. They live off money that was accumulated by someone else and passed on to them, and that fact defines the sort of person they become.

Until quite recently, the rentier in this more tightly defined sense was a recognized sociological figure, and one that entered significantly into analyses of the nature of modern capitalism. (Lenin saw the rentier as representative of capitalism in its imperialist stage.) But if the rentier was representative, it was also a source of moral and political confusion. Based on self-interest, Max Weber observed, rentiers ought to be hated by workers. But they aren't. Instead, workers tend to direct their anger at industrialists.

> It is not the rentier, the share-holder, and the banker who suffer the ill will of the worker, but almost exclusively the manufacturer and the business executives who are the direct opposites of workers in price wars. This is so in spite of the fact that it is precisely the cash boxes of the rentier, the share-holder, and the banker into which the more or less 'unearned' gains flow, rather than into the pockets of the manufacturers or the business executives.

Perversely, political emotion does *not* tend to follow the actual accumulation of money, even when the rentier's money might be perceived as more obviously unearned than the money of hard-working business executives.

That perversity seems relevant to contemporary anti-elitism, which is directed more at the educated than at the rich.[31] But it also suggests, even more perversely, the existence of a zone of tolerance in which the educated—say, economically noncompetitive academics and artists—might be protected from economic resentment. In his own time, Weber saw the concept of the rentier as necessary to explain the survival of artists and academics, at least to the extent that both are perceived as, at the same time, parasites and rebels: "Modern charismatic movements of artistic origin represent 'independents without gainful employment' (in everyday language, rentiers)."

The word *rentier* appears in George Orwell's much-admired essay on the novelist Charles Dickens. Orwell notices that Dickens, though he goes out of his way to remind Victorian readers of the poverty in their midst, doesn't often present characters at work. He links this disinclination to represent work with Dickens's penchant for characters who don't *have* to work—those who enjoy what was then called "an independence." Orwell expresses his disappointment that, with the possible exception of *David Copperfield*, "one cannot point to a single one of his central characters who is primarily interested in his job . . . The feeling, 'This is what I came into the world to do. Everything else is uninteresting. I will do this even if it means starvation,' which turns men of differing temperaments into scientists, inventors, artists, priests, explorers and revolutionaries—this motif is almost entirely absent from Dickens's books." When Orwell evokes the rentier, however, it is not as a mere antithesis of virtuous industry, hence a cheap target of ridicule. Rather, like Weber, he associates the figure with a certain political confusion. The rentier emerges in Dickens, he says, as a replacement for "the good rich man," a figure who "is usually a 'merchant,' and is always a superhumanly kind-hearted old gentleman who 'trots' to and fro, raising his employees' wages, patting children on the head, getting debtors out of jail and, in general, acting the fairy godmother. Of course he is a pure dream figure . . . Even Dickens must have reflected occasionally that anyone who was so anxious to give his money away would never have acquired it in the first place."

In the later, darker novels, Orwell goes on, "the good rich man has dwindled from a 'merchant' to a *rentier.* This is significant. A *rentier* is part of the possessing class, he can and, almost without knowing it, does make other people work for him, but he has very little direct power. Unlike Scrooge or the Cheerybles, he cannot put everything right by raising everybody's wages." Someone who cannot put everything right, though it is hinted that he might want to; someone who makes other people work for him, but not directly or consciously—these characteristics do not preclude satire, but they also suggest a more widely shared predicament, one with which Orwell himself seems to feel an uneasy intimacy. The situation of Dickens's rentier as Orwell sees him, well-intentioned but unable to perform the magic that would end the exploitation of which he is a reluctant beneficiary, neatly matches Orwell's account of the situation of his likely left-wing readers—and, though he is less clear on this point, his own situation as well. It has never been a secret that Orwell enjoyed a certain number of well-heeled benefactors, the sources of the money he lived on, though never luxuriously—those on whom his fierce intellectual independence depended.[32]

Orwell's portrait of the rentier would also fit the category of the full-time organizer or activist. Or politician, as Weber suggests. Weber famously argued in "Politics as a Vocation" that the politician would have to be a rentier, which is to say independently wealthy. This is not self-evident. Organizers, activists, and politicians need not be wealthy, and for the good of society probably should not be. Weber ignored the likelihood that being independently wealthy would give political leaders an interest in protecting and maintaining the state of society that generated their income. But he was right that they could not be expected to work a normal nine-to-five, five-days-a-week schedule and still perform the public duties that define them. The same holds for organizers, activists—and even students. Like the rentier, such social categories need to be supported, if only temporarily, out of some portion of society's economic surplus.

Who makes those decisions? Are they made invisibly by the market, or are they made in open, democratic discussion? How much money is distributed? These questions are inevitably controversial. But it is normal, which is to say uncontroversial, for some social categories or functions to be separated from paid wages. That is not necessarily an example of privilege.

For most people, most of the time, it has been and is still assumed that we have an obligation to take care of ourselves and those closest to us. As it approaches the extreme case of survival, this unarticulated common sense approaches the endpoint of amorality—caring for oneself by any means necessary, and therefore extending the same tolerance to others. When the issue is survival, the moral rules are suspended. Necessity makes its own rules. That's one reason why there are tacit limits to the questions we permit ourselves to ask about the source of other people's income *even when that income is inherited or otherwise unearned, hence open to question*. Rentiers benefit from the fact that working people give most people a pass because, it is assumed, where work is concerned most of us don't really have much choice.

For those of us who would like to see the hedge fund rentiers and those who make a living serving their needs held to moral account, the conclusion would seem to be that we must do whatever we can to ensure that survival is no longer an issue. The best name for this project has been and still is socialism. But for the moment, at least, steps in this direction can only be undertaken by the state, the state we have. It is ironic in the extreme, therefore, that another misguided political effect of the work ethic is anti-statism. I call this effect misguided because it's the state that has provided the best demonstration that yet exists that the link between paid work and moral worth can be broken. The name for this specific achievement is the welfare state, which has taken for its premise that no one should have to fear for their survival, whether because of the vagaries of the job market or for any other reason. Beggars can't be choosers.

The goal is that there should be no beggars in order that everyone can be a chooser. We need more of this project, not less. We need the state to regulate the financial industry, to render financial instruments transparent, including those that permit investment in militarism, to tax financial transactions—and perhaps also to introduce a serious inheritance tax, thereby leveling the playing field of work and thereby reinvesting work with meaning. And we need the state to diminish as far as possible that amoral sense of ultimate responsibility for our own survival that likewise protects the energetic inventors of toxic derivatives.

I am not suggesting that artists, intellectuals, and scholars of literature, looking at the rentier, should recognize themselves. My point is that they or we can better avoid such a guilty recognition to the extent that we can feel better about the way society's surplus has been allocated. The less democratic the decision-making—that is, the more that surplus is distributed by the market or by inheritance—the fainter the ethical border separating students and professors from the lucky children of hedge fund founders. The closer that process comes to being conducted by economic as well as formal equals, the better its beneficiaries can feel. There are more persuasive motives for socialism than the quest for an untroubled conscience, but no good motive should be neglected.

TWO

AT LEAST MODEST COMFORT

Artists and writers are of course not the only ones who hesitate to disclose how they earn a livelihood. But their hesitation seems more palpable to us, perhaps because those ways of earning a living are supposed to be about something higher than earning a living; sometimes they are understood, rightly or wrongly, to embody the ideal of dissent. It's as if it were agreed in advance, armed with this suspicion, that the motive for asking the "what does X live on ?" question could only be malicious in its essence, a seemingly innocent appeal for information that would eventually serve to fuel spiteful commentary. It's upsetting to think that the highest reward for following the money may be nothing more than access to malicious gossip. *De Quoi Vivait Gérard de Nerval* belongs to a series that came out through the 1950s and answered the "what did he live on?" question for Molière, Voltaire, Balzac, Dostoyevsky, and Tolstoy. The aim of the series was clearly not to embellish the authors' aura of greatness.[1]

On the other hand, why did I go to the library in search of the Nerval book? Does curiosity on the subject of how writers earned a living have to be resentful or otherwise mean-spirited? Is knowledge on this subject inherently accusatory? Whether the achievement in question is artistic or political, it doesn't seem right that the accused should be considered guilty until they can prove that they are on the brink of starvation.

The students in the Gaza encampments were not starving—fair enough. In general, observers who link student protest with privilege are not incorrect. In relation to the public at large, students are indeed a privileged group.[2] That much would be readily conceded by student protesters themselves. It was already conceded by the framers of the Port Huron Statement in 1962, which established the guidelines for Students for a Democratic Society, the group that went on to spearhead the Columbia protests in 1968 and the Harvard protests in 1969. The first sentence of the Port Huron Statement reads: "We are people of this generation, bred in at least modest comfort, housed now in universities, looking uncomfortably to the world we inherit."[3] This statement recognizes that being admitted to universities is a privilege not shared with the rest of their generation, and it recognizes even more emphatically that, economically speaking, the background for their political discomfort is "at least modest comfort." It's a meaningful and self-consciously uncomfortable phrase.

You can glimpse both the at least modestly comfortable origins of the student radicals and their discomfort with those origins in a sort of primal scene recorded by participant-and-later-sociologist Richard Flacks. The scene occurs at a convention of SDS, the Port Huron group. It's another scene of awkward fundraising. "Toward the end of several days of deliberation, someone decided that a quick way of raising funds for the organization would be to appeal to the several hundred students assembled at the convention to dig down deep into their pockets on the spot. To this end, one of the leadership, skilled at mimicry, stood on a chair, and in the style of a Southern Baptist preacher, appealed to the students to come forward, confess their sins and be saved by contributing to SDS. The students did come forward, and in each case the sin confessed was the social class or occupation of their fathers. 'My father is the editor of a Hearst newspaper, I give $25'! 'My father is Assistant Director of the Bureau, I give $40.' 'My father is dean of a law school, here's $50'!" These impressions of the social composition of the student movement, Flacks goes on, are supported and refined by more systematic sources of data.[4]

No one involved in this role-playing would seem to have been fully committed to the analogy between social privilege and sin or between salvation and making a financial pledge. The smiles are not recorded, but they would have been inevitable. Also unrecorded are those in attendance who might not have had a father's occupation worthy of mention or the money to pledge in recompense. What is clear is that some privilege is an uncomfortable fact about that gathering, a fact that had to be dealt with. In his best-selling book *The Sixties: Years of Hope, Days of Rage*, which begins with the word affluence, Todd Gitlin summarizes the complex feelings illustrated in Flacks's scene in two interrelated structural premises.

> Premise #1: "The New Left's torment—the torment of all radical student movements—was that relatively privileged people were fighting on behalf of the oppressed: blacks, Vietnamese, the working class."
>
> Premise #2: "The working class was conservative, more or less, the privileged were radical."[5]

In other words, though Black people and the Vietnamese were of course also fighting, and there were links of different sorts between the students and those collectivities (in the case of Black people, both overlap and active alliance), the students were not themselves the oppressed for whom they were fighting. The crucial piece that was missing, for Gitlin, was the working class, which is here presented as not fighting.

Another anecdote illustrates this consciousness of a broken link between student privilege and the unprivileged working class and, perhaps, therefore, "the torment of all radical student movements." That scene is the so-called

Hard Hat Riot on May 8, 1970. Students were demonstrating against the Vietnam War in Lower Manhattan. Construction workers in hard hats, some of them engaged in building the nearby World Trade Center, arrived and started beating the students. The police of course stood by or joined in. For some of us who were students at the time, it seemed that a line had been drawn through the left, with anti-war activists on one side and the organized labor movement, faithful supporters of the US military, on the other. Highlighting that divide was the fact that four days earlier, peaceful student demonstrators had been shot and killed by the Ohio National Guard at Kent State. From a student's perspective, the optics for this springtime display of working-class patriotism were not ideal.

History has suggested that this student-versus-labor opposition was not as simple as it seemed at the time. The point can be made, again, by following the money trail. The meeting at Port Huron where the famous SDS statement was drafted and debated happened at a labor education camp, which had been loaned to the students by the United Auto Workers. SDS did not get all its funding from the guilty sons of prosperous fathers. In addition, it also received considerable funding from Walter Reuther, president of the UAW.[6] And this makes sense. If you look at Reuther's speeches, you find considerable common ground between the student activists and the labor movement.

As it happens, May 9, 1970, the day after the Hard Hat Riot, is also the day when Walter Reuther died in a plane crash. It's possible that he was assassinated; a previous assassination attempt had failed. Not long afterward real wages for non-college-educated workers began to decline. That decline and its consequences are the big political story of our age, in some ways the story that will continue to be ours as long as the Democrats continue to make themselves the party of Wall Street and the college educated. It's the story of the Hard Hat Riot writ large. It is certainly a much bigger story than the sequence of post-boomer generations whose names and supposed sensibilities have so preoccupied the columnists and advertisers.

But the story still has some twists and turns in it. Reuther joined the Cold War crusade against Communism, and his personal critique of the war in Vietnam, shared by others in the UAW, never became an official UAW position. On the other hand, his early environmentalism found an echo in Shawn Fain's reinvigorated UAW. And more than a quarter of the members of Reuther's union now work in higher education. The UAW represents Columbia's graduate students and teaching assistants, who are much more vocal than their elders against US and Israeli militarism. History has not come full circle—it never does—but it seems some loose ends are getting tied up, some links are getting articulated, and a supposedly unbridgeable chasm between more and less privileged is being crossed.

In 1970, I was unaware that a recent book of sociology had helped explain my own complicated feelings of hope and inertia, and the situation in the world to which those feelings corresponded. In 1969, Immanuel Wallerstein published *University in Turmoil*, a book inspired by the protests at Columbia. When the protests broke out in April 1968, Wallerstein had been teaching for a decade in Columbia's department of sociology. He had received tenure on the strength of three books about the politics of a newly independent Africa. His own politics could be described, in the lexicon of the day, as Third Worldist. The same could be said of some, though not all, of the Columbia protesters, who were indignant both at an attempted land grab by the university in Harlem and at its many-sided complicity with American militarism in Vietnam and elsewhere. Wallerstein was on the students' side. But he was a faculty member, not a student. It must have felt awkward to be a professor when students were the ones calling the shots and taking the risks, but when the university as an institution also seemed to be at risk. Like Edward W. Said, his colleague in the department of English and comparative literature who was to expand radically the zone of the sayable about Palestine, Wallerstein held publicly unpopular views and clearly treasured the protection that the university provided.

The language of *University in Turmoil* will probably strike today's reader as dispassionate—indeed, colorless to the point of anemia. The preface calls the book "the fruit of an intensely personal experience," but the personal and the intensity have been scrubbed away, at least from the prose. Instead of the activists' inflammatory rage—to the less accommodating, their sloganizing and bluster—Wallerstein opts for neutral-sounding abstractions and a calm sociological detachment. He does not permit himself to mention, say, the victims of Operation Rolling Thunder (1965–68), the bombing campaign against North Vietnam that by itself probably killed as many Vietnamese civilians as the total number of American casualties in the war. It's as if he is trying not to sound like the protesters themselves even when he is in wholehearted agreement with them.

With Gaza's mass graves silently screaming in their ears, readers today will perhaps wonder whether Wallerstein's reluctance to make any noise about death in Vietnam was too well-mannered, and thus also whether it is a model to be avoided now. Some will no doubt suspect Wallerstein of sacrificing his political commitments on the altar of academic autonomy. He could reply that the choice, as he sees it, is not so simple. Is his employer working hand in glove with the war machine? It is. Is he himself nevertheless loyal to the university as an idea and an ideal? Yes again. It's in the name of an ideally denationalized universality that he asserts the right to scrutinize and perhaps reject the university's collaborations with the government. Such scrutiny is entirely fitting and proper, he suggests, for an academic citizen. The university, properly conceived, is a political institution, a place of both intellectual and social conflict. Conflict is what he is engaging in. You may think it impossible to remain civil while arguing that your colleagues, under cover of intellectual autonomy, are defending a murderous status quo. If so, watch and learn. That's one moral of his performance.

In his introduction to *Student Power*, coedited with Robin Blackburn and also published in 1969, Alexander Cockburn wrote: "The emergence of the student movement promises a renewal of revolutionary politics as well as the arrival of a new social force." For Cockburn, "student insurgents," rejecting parliamentary politics, are that new revolutionary social force.[7] For Wallerstein, becoming a revolutionary force is more than students can justifiably claim. "Insurrection . . . makes no sense as a tactic of university reform as long as the university exists within a reasonably enduring political system." The fact that the American working class is relatively conservative, for example about the war in Vietnam, ought not to be surprising; deprived as they are within the United States, seen from an international perspective they benefit from America's place in the global capitalist system. Globally considered, they are among the privileged. And for the same reason, the American university cannot be turned into a revolutionary institution. Trying to make the US "a bastion of world revolution" is "a non-issue and nonsense." The same holds for America's organized working class as for the American university. The university is and will remain "a bastion of the center . . . kept squarely in the center and in tension with the right because of the strength of the left." In other words, it will never be a bastion of the left, and if the student radicals try to push it in that direction, things will not end well. What the university can be for the left is what it turned out to be for him, as for Edward Said and Noam Chomsky: a "refuge and a point of sortie."

If the university is and will likely remain a bastion of the center in a society that is itself centrist at best, globally speaking, what can the student protests reasonably hope for? They should not hope for significant support from a majority of the faculty. And they cannot expect to have much impact on what Wallerstein calls, in an awkward sociologism, "resource allocation"—that is, the revolutionary goal of economic justice at a global scale. *At the global scale, both American students and the American working class have to count as economically privileged.*[8] They have that in common. The differences between them are very real, but they can't be reduced to privilege versus nonprivilege. Privilege too is real, but at the metropolitan center it is widely shared.

In 1970, I was probably not alone, among anti-war students contemplating the Hard Hat Riot, in thinking that from a global perspective we were more faithful representatives of the working class than the construction workers. The global working class was living under military dictatorships supported by the US. The global working class was scrambling to take what shelter it could from American bombs. It was having its surplus siphoned off and transferred to the metropolis, where some of it was passed around to forestall worker dissent. In 1974, Wallerstein's world-systems theory would lay all this out, including the official US labor movement's general support for US imperialism, thereby providing theoretical cover for what was essentially middle-class radicalism.

This argument will not inspire many young activists to get up and put their bodies on the line. It speaks less to the burning motives for activism than to its discouraging limits. Yet it makes an exception for organized outrage at the war in Vietnam. For Wallerstein, the violence in Vietnam had already achieved a shift of the center to the left. Organizationally speaking, it is a success story, and this is true even if it is not (what Wallerstein wants most) a major blow against global economic inequality. Violence speaks in a resonant voice, and that is arguably the most relevant aspect of Wallerstein's account of 1968 for the pro-Palestinian demonstrators of 2024.

Kelman, Brooks, and the others are wrong, therefore, in imagining that they can refute student radicalism by pointing to the relative privileges of its adherents. It is no surprise that they should all be so vague about what exactly these privileges consist of. They don't *want* to know; to look closely at those supposed privileges, to follow the money, might show that they were not after all so very privileged or luxurious. That would throw cold water on their fiery rhetoric. But for the moment I will maintain their indistinctness. For the moment, it's enough to say that, morally and politically, having *some* money is not the same thing as having *too much* money. In any case, decisions about which side to take require more than knowing the source or size of someone's bank balance.

"At least modest comfort," the phrase that opens the Port Huron Statement, does not put the category of student protesters into the one percent. Grace Elizabeth Hale, looking back on that opening sentence, commented that, for the framers of the statement, the world was presented as "not oppressive or unjust but 'uncomfortable'. . . Coupled with the phrase 'modest comfort' and the verb 'housed,' 'uncomfortable' implies the feeling people who are not accustomed to unpleasantness experience—people of a generation, yes, but also of a particular class."[9] True enough, but it was not irrelevant that the discomfort made it impossible to enjoy one's privileged place in the social system. Gitlin goes on in *The Sixties* to conclude: "We, the collectively privileged . . . could not be trusted."[10] This untrustworthiness is close to the voice of the paradigmatic French student radical, as ventriloquized by Berman: "I am privileged, therefore I am nothing."

On reflection, the word comfort is an interesting alternative to this absolutism. Perhaps it deserves a bigger place in the discourse of the left. In *The Bourgeois: Between History and Literature*, Franco Moretti connects the word's history, unsurprisingly, to the history of the bourgeoisie.[11] Initially, comfort indicated relief from some sort of physical or mental distress. By the late seventeenth century, however, "comfort is no longer what returns us to a 'normal' state from adverse circumstances. But what takes normality as its starting point *and pursues well-being as an end in itself*, independently of any mishap." Comfort thus falls somewhere between necessities and luxuries. Or, with reference to *Robinson Crusoe*, whose proudest comforts are a simple table and a simple chair, comfort might be located closer to necessity: "Luxury is always somewhat out of the ordinary; comfort, never; whence the profound common sense of its pleasures." Comfort is better described as "everyday necessities made pleasant." Hence the earlier dictionary sense of comfort as relief returns, this time not as relief from sickness but as relief from work, which is assumed to be the normal condition, and a taxing one. There is a recognition here of the desire for pleasure, but the recognition is minimal, suited to the asceticism of Weber's Protestant work ethic. For better or worse, there is no recognition of the desire for superiority—Bourdieu's theme—over anyone else. This is bourgeois ideology, granted, but it arguably does more to explain middle-class activism than the Bourdieu-inspired hypothesis that derives activism from gloating about your superior status.

In the interest of supplying some nuance about the privilege of students, much could be said about student debt—larger than mortgage or credit card debt—and general precarity; about how many students, and how many student demonstrators, are on food stamps, or are eligible for food stamps but too proud or too inept to apply for food stamps, or are kept from eligibility for food stamps by regulations like the requirement of a twenty-hour-a-week job that might prevent them from ever finishing their studies.[12] Caitlin Zaloom has painstakingly documented the sacrifices made by middle-class families to put and keep a child in college.[13] There exist, no doubt, trust fund hipsters and, by extension, trust fund intellectuals. But there are also food stamp hipsters and food stamp intellectuals. And there are many students, artists, and writers who, falling between trust funds and food stamps, really ought not to be dismissed as elites, as if they spent their time hobnobbing with Supreme Court justices and managers of private equity firms.

Terms like cultural elite and liberal elite do a lot of work in contemporary political discourse, and the assumption is that, despite a certain imprecision, everyone knows well enough what they mean. In many cases, however, it's their vagueness that makes them so efficacious. They are vague about one thing in particular: about whether power resides in the possession of wealth. As we know, wealth buys lobbyists, legislation, tax loopholes, presidencies.

What power can't it buy? But elite, in its frequent polemical usages, suggests that power is not really in the hands of the super-wealthy. It is in the hands of the highly educated or highly cultivated. Elite displaces the location of power from money to education or cultivation. It makes the money disappear, or at any rate discourages the politically curious from following it too closely.[14]

This seems to be true, mysteriously, even when elitism and elites are criticized from the left. In *Twilight of the Elites: Prosperity, the Periphery, and the Future of France*, Christophe Guilluy takes aim not so much at "the dominant class" as "the large segment of society" who support the dominant class. That segment includes "those who gain from globalization," but also those who, though they might not gain, "are protected from [globalization's] adverse consequences)."[15] In other words, perhaps they have not suffered acutely enough. Like the idea of support for the dominant class, the criterion of insufficient suffering widens the category dangerously. As does the crucial specification that follows: Members of this stratum, though they are "privileged," "need not be either rich or owners of capital."

It is no wonder, then, to see the target of Guilluy's critique skidding from the possessors of money to the possessors of something he calls, repeatedly, coolness. The gilet jaune movement in France "has shaken the moral certainties of the self-styled 'cool' bourgeoisie, sure of its own benevolence." His ire burns hottest against "affluent hipsters," or "the new gentrifiers" when they are "disguised as hipsters." It's much the same slide away from money in Catherine Liu's *Virtue Hoarders: The Case Against the Professional Managerial Class.*[16] As her title suggests, what enrages Liu is not the hoarding of money but the hoarding of virtue, the supposed point of which (she cites David Brooks, of course) is to distinguish those who do so from the uncredentialed working class. Like the Bernsteins' living room as seen by Wolfe, Buckley, and Brooks, it's all about the elite insisting on their superior status. The problem is not that you are not paid a decent wage; it's that "they" look down on you. Looking down on you is what "they" really want. The real problem is not money, which is objective, but entitlement, which is subjective.

Whatever the incoherences in their arguments, these writers are notable for the genuine intensity of the feelings they represent, feelings that are undoubtedly widely shared, though (as I'm trying to suggest) they are also misdirected. In other words, the kind of mistake they make is also widely shared. It's of a piece with the meaning of elite in Michael M. Grynbaum's *Empire of the Elite: Inside Condé Nast, the Media Dynasty That Reshaped America.*[17] When Grynbaum talks about the glamorous editors of large-circulation glossies like *Vogue* and the glamorous people they interviewed, photographed, and had long lunches with, what he means by the elite is the glamorous. According to Grynbaum, SI Newhouse, the inheritor of a huge fortune, measured the success of his treasured magazines in terms of circulation, not profit. He was content to lose money, as his magazines often did, if he and his buzz-creating magazines remained the coolest kids on the block. There is nothing to stop this aspirational picture of the elite from shifting back into Wolfe's politically mobilized class-resentment picture, which was never very far from it to begin with.

In Brooks's sketch of recent social history, culture and education are supposed to have acquired social, economic, and political power.[18] Have they? Yes, there is a large disparity of lifetime incomes between those with and without higher degrees. But does higher education confer real power? Brooks doesn't say so explicitly. If he did, he would have to include himself not just among the bobos, where he is clearly happy to take his seat, but among the powerful. Perhaps he would even have to locate himself in the ruling class. For his readers, assigning himself to the ruling class would be less ingratiating. It might even be the end of his column. (Imagine Musk, Zuckerberg, or Bezos with a column in the *Times*.) It's hard to tell whether Brooks's indecision on this point is politically calculating or merely confused. "In this era," he writes, "ideas and knowledge are at least as vital to economic success as natural resources and finance capital." At least as? That would imply that what "ideas and knowledge" confer is equal to the power conferred by the possession of finance capital, actual money. Or perhaps that "ideas and knowledge" are now even *more* "vital" than the possession of finance capital. Is it possible that for Brooks, "economic success" *doesn't* mean power? Brooks won't quite say that today the well-educated hold society's reins, that they are not merely setters of cultural fashions but the new ruling class. But the phrase "new upper class," in the book's subtitle, suggests exactly that. Ditto for Brooks's commentary on the *New York Times* weddings page (he cleverly calls it "mergers and acquisitions"), which claims that the elect are no longer defined by "noble birth and breeding" but by "genius and geniality."[19]

The sprinkling of qualifiers that have recently been added to contemporary capitalism, like information, service, and surveillance, each suggesting with a certain cognitive kick that capitalism has now assumed some wholly new form, have the side effect of suggesting that the location of power has shifted in some significant way. They often tend to suggest, to be more precise, that real power is now exercised by knowledge workers, creatives, and possessors of information. This is questionable. Yes, as we have heard, some people have made a lot of money in IT, and more money will no doubt be made. But if there is creativity in the work of the educated elite, at least sometimes, creativity is not the same as the power to make decisions, like the decision to merge or acquire.[20] Even Brooks can see that control is a different thing. When he notes, toward the end of the book, that "*they* are an elite based above all on education" (my italics), this "they" refers to an educated subgroup, not to society's actual rulers. In other words, he is backing off his earlier and more incendiary claim. Here he concedes that being "an elite based above all on education," whatever else it may entail, does not in fact bestow decisive wealth or decisive power. Those with wealth and power are a much more exclusive group.

It doesn't seem coincidental that the term elite and the discipline of sociology came into circulation at roughly the same time, in the late nineteenth century.[21] It was early sociologists like Vilfredo Pareto, Gaetano Mosca, and Robert Michels who popularized it.[22] According to Google Ngram, it was not until the 1960s that elite was much used in English. Then it was suddenly everywhere. In other words, it is only in the last six or seven decades that the term has flourished, and it seems plausible that it has done so because it has served as a tool of large-scale political misdirection. This was the period in the United States of the Reagan Democrats, the period when the Democratic Party was losing its traditional white working-class constituency. In this period, channeling anger toward elites has allowed the Republican Party and its corporate funders to hide the real power of money—their own money, and that of the Wall Street wing of the Democratic Party—behind the putative power of education (for example, the power to encourage secularism and wokeness) and the contempt supposedly felt by the educated elite for the uneducated. Without this vocabulary, the landscape of American politics today would be unrecognizable.

But if educated elites have in fact seized power, how much power have they seized? Or does the word elite simply indicate those who unquestionably *have* power, whether they attained it by means of education or by the more traditional means of money, birth, or family connections? In its European origins, the concept of the elite helped sponsor a bourgeois power grab against, or in compromise with, the hereditary aristocracy. According to Christophe Charle, the concept emerged in late nineteenth century France as part of a political effort to legitimate a new ruling class in terms of enlightenment rather than birth and wealth. The effort failed: It was "too aristocratic for the democrats, too enlightened for the Catholic conservatives."[23] Charle does not pretend that higher education was an essential constituent of the period's ruling class; for him it was only how some of its members tried to present themselves.[24] Fritz Ringer, writing about Germany during these same years, sees the same effort as succeeding, but only briefly. He defines his "mandarins" (Max Weber is the most famous example) as "a social and cultural elite which owes its status primarily to educational qualifications rather than to hereditary rights or wealth."[25] Ringer includes "doctors, lawyers, ministers, government officials, secondary school teachers, and university professors, all of them men with advanced academic degrees based on the completion of a certain minimum curriculum and the passing of a conventional group of examinations." How much power did the "mandarins" really have? Ringer vacillates. He says they achieved "a predominant role within their society," and then in the next sentence he calls them "a functional ruling class." A functional ruling class has a great deal of power. On the other hand, if the "mandarins" ever had real power, they certainly didn't keep it for long. Ringer specifies that they could become a functional ruling class only "under certain specific conditions," that is, during a particular phase in the material development of their country. They thrive between the primarily agrarian level of economic organization and full industrialization. At that intermediate stage, the ownership of significant amounts of liquid capital has not yet become either widespread or widely accepted as a qualification for social status." In other words, the stage of mandarin-elite power has long been over. And in that case, usage of the term elite continues to conceal the fact that power has reverted to the possessors of "liquid capital," or what Mike Savage calls "the wealth elite."[26]

The big story behind contemporary references both to elites and to meritocracy, the system that supposedly elevated them, is a vanishing act performed on liquid capital, that is, money. American meritocracy has been denounced, left, right, and center, for its production or reproduction of elites who believe, falsely, that they have earned their privilege. If the issue is indeed a matter of elite *belief*, then it would be worth distinguishing between privilege, which is objective, and entitlement, which is also a belief, an attitude. The belief that you *deserve* the privileges that the system in its wisdom has bestowed on you is a real problem; it makes the system itself seem just, which it is not. But entitlement can take other forms. It can also take the form of cynicism, or nihilism. The cynical or nihilistic version would go something like this: "No one truly deserves what the system allocates them. The system is random and meaningless. But if so, then I might as well enjoy the privileges I have been born with or otherwise allocated." That is arguably the conclusion that best aligns with the embarrassment-avoiding zone of polite amoral tolerance that rules out asking "what does X live on?" This cynicism or nihilism seems philosophically advanced. Maybe, but it's also part of the fortifications that protect economic inequality. There's a reason why it is so widespread: It's paid for.

Communitarian political theorist Michael Sandel describes meritocracy, simply and persuasively, as "a justification of inequality."[27] That real economic inequality has persisted and increased is not news. No politics that does not address it is worth anyone's attention. It remains remarkable, however, that denunciations of privileged elites have managed, by focusing their critique on education and on the meritocracy's complacent self-belief, to ignore the primary cause for the increase in monetary inequality: money itself.[28]

Indeed, the effect of much of the scolding has been, perversely, to launder the money. For Christopher Lasch in *The Revolt of the Elites*, one of the problems with the "new elites" produced by meritocracy, professionalism, and "the selective promotion of non-elites into the professional-managerial class" is "the decline of old money and the old-money ethic of civic responsibility." Lasch remembers old money with some fondness: "Philanthropy implicated elites in the lives of their neighbors and in those of generations to come."[29] For Andrew Delbanco, as for Lasch, the underlying claim is not just that the new, more diverse meritocracy is still hierarchical, but that things were better when power was in the hands of the old money. In *College: What It Was, Is, and Should Be*, Delbanco suggests that the possessors of old money were morally superior because they saw their wealth as unearned, accidental. The old (Protestant) religion taught the old, moneyed elite, very properly, "the principle that no human being deserves anything based on his or her merit."[30] Delbanco quotes conservative columnist Ross Douthat: It was "God (or blind chance)" that "had given the elite much that was not necessarily deserved." Hence the money came with a responsibility to give back. The new meritocratic elite, on the other hand, believes it deserves its privileges; hence it thinks it can look down on those who have not earned those privileges through talent and hard work. It doesn't owe anyone anything. Those who hold that belief are probably not reading this essay, but if by chance one is, read on. It is questionable whether pre-meritocratic beliefs were really any better—whether the old religion taught, and whether old money ever learned, that the acquisition of wealth was accidental rather than, on the contrary, a sign of godliness in the wealthy. Late in life the robber barons often gave a lot of money away, but this doesn't mean most of them should be seen as acting responsibly.[31]

Seeing responsibility laid out as a supposed virtue of the old, pre-meritocratic elites, one is tempted to stop and ask a perverse question. If responsibility may in fact *be* a political virtue, if we think our society needs and wants more responsibility even if we don't want the old money back in charge, then where do we think responsibility could come from, socially speaking? It can't come only from old money. Could it also be a virtue of the modestly comfortable?

Progressives have not shown much curiosity about this question, and the reason is obvious. Answering it would seem to entail giving in to the persistence of what is still being called privilege, and that admission would undercut the basic progressive assumption that political agency must always come from below, even from as far below as possible. Thus it would be bound to provoke some unease.[32] But consider Noam Chomsky's 1966 essay, "The Responsibility of Intellectuals," a powerful anti-war polemic based not on the sixties slogan of identity but on no-double-standards universalism. The only concession to identity Chomsky made, you might say, was to the privileged identity of the educated, which he didn't want his educated readers to abandon. The privilege came with a special obligation, Chomsky argued, to fight militarism using the capacities and access that the system had given them, unfairly and mistakenly, and had not given to others. You don't want to give those arms away. Chomsky's essay was a major influence on Edward W. Said—not coincidentally, an intellectual who was sometimes chided for his familial and Upper West Side privilege.[33]

In her denunciation of the professional-managerial class as virtue hoarders, Catherine Liu pauses to take issue with the rosier view of that class by Gabriel Winant: "Winant believes in liberal virtue; I do not." Unfortunately for her, her belief in the virtue of the class she is denouncing is built into the structure of her argument. She argues that the PMC has betrayed itself. But it can only have betrayed itself if, before its supposed effort to flaunt its difference from the poor below it, it saw itself as on the same side as the poor. And that is indeed what Liu's decline story posits: once upon a time, the PMC "sympathized with the plight of masses of working people," and "it was after 1968 that the PMC gradually shifted its allegiance from workers to capital ... When the tide turned against American workers, the PMC preferred to fight culture wars against the classes below while currying favor of capitalists it once despised." Or rather, it's only "the most successful and visible segments of the PMC" that have done so.

There is some truth in these charges, of course, but there is also evidence in favor of Gabriel Winant's more optimistic view of the possibilities for middle-class radicalism, what Liu calls "liberal virtue," or what might also be called responsibility. Winant writes: "The PMC is not the ruling class, it merely serves it, deliberately or inadvertently. In this way, professionals do share something with the working class, which is why it is possible to imagine their realignment with working class interests: they share the lack of ultimate control over their conditions of labor."[34] In 2013, two years after Occupy Wall Street, Barbara and John Ehrenreich, the originators of the term professional-managerial class, updated their argument. A "renewal of oppositional spirit among the Professional-Managerial Class, or what remains of it," was by no means impossible, they proposed, as long as it began from an awareness that what has happened to the professional middle class has long since happened to the blue-collar working class. Those of us who have college and higher degrees have proved to be no more indispensable, as a group, to the American capitalist enterprise than those who honed their skills on assembly lines or in warehouses or foundries. The debt-ridden unemployed and underemployed college graduates, the revenue-starved teachers, the overworked and underpaid service professionals, even the occasional whistle-blowing scientist or engineer—all face the same kind of situation that confronted skilled craft-workers in the early twentieth century and all

American industrial workers in the late twentieth century.[35]

Winant, quoting these lines, adds that this has in fact been happening:

> Professional-class activists have found something in their own indignities on the job to connect them to the broader working class: teachers and nurses have articulated their own demands in terms of solidarity with the students and patients they serve; tech workers first practiced protest in solidarity with security guards and bus drivers on their campuses, before finding they needed it themselves. Our organizing of unions and strikes in the last years, our refusals to build technology for the military-industrial complex and carceral state, our assertions of solidarity in the common struggle against sexual harassment and assault in school and at work, and yes, our electoral campaigns, including the Sanders campaigns—all these mark the advancement of this project.

Responsibility often seems restricted to what has come to be called, with a strong hint of fake democracy, stakeholders. The term is tainted, and it is right and proper to suspect that its only function is to conceal inequality of actual ownership and the unequal control that stems from it. But if a sense of ownership is a *sine qua non*, it does not follow that the ownership is necessarily unequal. The fact that ownership has so often been a zero-sum game does not mean that it must be. The same for power. Taking a responsibility upon yourself entails conceding only that you possess some degree of power to carry out your wishes. If you didn't think you *could* carry them out, you wouldn't feel the responsibility to try. If you want to change the world, desiring the tools needed to change it—that is, the power to change it—should not be too painful a concession.

I say this at the risk of seeming to want to whitewash the power of money. And to some extent, with some qualifications, that *is* what I want. I hope the qualifications will be clear. In any case, some moral revisionism must be allowed if we are to keep the focus on money as a weapon of the superrich and stop it from encouraging spiteful and misleading references to educated or credentialed or cultural elites. I assume that the most significant social injustices are those that come from the maldistribution of money, not the maldistribution of education; that the grossest, most unjust part of the maldistribution of education is determined by the gross, unjust distribution of money; and that the maldistribution of money determines the maldistribution of power. What I want is to try to get the power of money back in proper political focus, which includes legitimizing the desire for and the possession of *some* of it. To repeat, perhaps tiresomely: Starvation is not an option. Subsistence is not an ideal. Having some leisure to read and reflect, discuss and organize, is a precondition for any effective participatory politics.[36]

It might even be helpful, though it would certainly be dangerous, to consider retrieving as a goal, alongside "at least modest comfort," the old term competence, meaning both expertise (the present meaning) and basic economic security (the older meaning).[37] If the term is indeed worth trying to resuscitate, the point of it would be that having competence need not signify having a position that is either unwarranted or (depending on the comparison) grossly and unjustly privileged. As it stands now, having some training in distinguishing true statements from false statements is indeed a privilege, as Chomsky suggests in that essay, and it is a privilege that arguably incurs political responsibilities. That this privilege requires funding ought not to be a scandal. The scandal is that, like the dignity that goes with them, such privileges are unequally distributed. Anti-elitism, by laundering the power of large sums of money, freezes that inequality in place.

In *The Big Test: The Secret History of the American Meritocracy*, Nicholas Lemann argues (as the jacket copy says) that the Educational Testing Service aimed "to create a new democratic elite" that would "unseat the quasi-hereditary male white elite that had run America." The originators of meritocracy believed, Lemann writes, "they were destroying a nascent class system and building a fluid, mobile society. In retrospect, this was vainglorious—you can't undermine social rank by setting up an elaborate process of ranking. Fifty years later, their creation looks more and more like what it was intended to replace." Meritocracy has produced the same inequality that it purported to supersede.

Lemann may want to complain about the residual power of family money to determine rank, but what he objects to explicitly is something different. It's ranking as such, ranking by any measure. He qualifies this objection, noting that he does not balk at the elite conceived as those with the capacity to fill "positions of authority and expertise." On the other hand, he does object to the idea of "general worth, as if [elites] were an updated Puritan elect." It would be best, he concludes, simply to abandon the category of the elite. But if the category cannot be removed from circulation completely, the next best solution, in Lemann's view, would be to eliminate the accompanying sense of moral worth, restricting the term instead to "access to jobs with specific functions." In other words, elite status should not be allowed to serve as "a ticket to lifelong prestige, comfort, and safety."

This formulation may seem promisingly democratic, but on second glance it is a good deal less attractive. Comfort, at least long-term comfort, is explicitly disallowed. Wouldn't society be better off if there were prestige, comfort, and safety for, say, air traffic controllers and environmental inspectors? In Lemann's brave new world, "there would be as little lifelong tenure on the basis of youthful promise as possible. The elite would be a group with a constantly shifting rather than a stable and permanent membership. Successful people would have less serene careers, but this would give them more empathy for people whose lives don't go smoothly." If one is plotting out a more just society, empathy for people who don't have access to the most desirable jobs is no doubt commendable, but it is much, much less than one should be requesting. In effect, what Lemann is requesting is neoliberalism. Like neoliberalism's champions, he wants to rule out considerations of "moral worth." That seems emancipatory—as neoliberalism seemed to Foucault. Unfortunately, like the neoliberals, he also wants to rule out serenity and security. Lemann asks, like the neoliberals, for a fuller marketization or adjunctification of society. Money, old or new, will now be making all the staffing decisions. Administrators, in the university as well as the government, have no doubt found much to appreciate in the proposal.[38]

In the face of this closet neoliberalism, let us try returning to some basic, once-uncontroversial assumptions. Sociology is correct that society exists. Society cannot be equated with the market. For its own reasons, or when pushed, society may decide to allocate funds to enterprises, like art, that are not immediately profitable or, like critical thinking, may make their contribution to the general welfare only in the long run. Allocation is not injustice; it depends on how that allocation happens. On that series of assumptions, following the money people live on may lead to something other than exposés like Jane Mayer's *Dark*

Money or Frances Stonor Saunders's *The Cultural Cold War: The CIA and the World of Arts and Letters*.[39] The exposé is a necessary and deeply satisfying genre, and there are never enough exposés—certainly not enough on the high level of Mayer and Stonor Saunders. Still, the exposé cannot be the only genre that answers the question of "what does X live on," be X a person, a demonstration, a state agency, or a little magazine.

THREE

WHAT DO LITTLE MAGAZINES LIVE ON?

Nineteenth-century bohemia would not have worked as Bourdieu says it worked without inherited fortunes. And Bourdieu himself says so. Having defined nineteenth-century bohemia by its rejection of the marketplace, he concedes that inheritances were necessary to its functioning. He recognizes that the role of inheritance was determining and, more surprisingly still, in his eyes, that its effect was globally positive. "As in *Sentimental Education*, 'inheritors' hold a decisive advantage when it comes to pure art: inherited economic capital, which removes the constraints and demands of immediate needs . . . and makes it possible to 'hold on' in the absence of a market, is one of the most important factors in the differential success of avant-garde enterprises." The point is not, after all, whether symbolic capital can eventually be converted into economic capital. It's that you don't have the ability to generate symbolic capital in the first place unless you have a private income or—like Nerval—have inherited a small fortune: "It is once again money (inherited) that guarantees freedom with respect to money. All the more so since, in giving assurances, guarantees, and safety nets, a fortune confers that audacity which fortune smiles on—without doubt more in matters of art than anywhere else." You need money, Bourdieu admits, in order to be fortunate enough to ignore money—or more precisely, to take some distance from the values of the marketplace.[1]

The advantages that those who come from family money enjoy in the worlds of art and literature have not disappeared. Nor have the troubled feelings that go with starting out at a major disadvantage, feelings experienced by those not born to money or socialized to it or otherwise made to feel that they don't belong to its world. No doubt it is no less infuriating now than it must have been then to the would-be artist or writer in nineteenth-century Paris who did not have money behind them and therefore had to give up their aspirations and perhaps be labeled a failure.

Bourdieu, who himself had none of these advantages, nevertheless ascribes a positive and determining role to familial inheritance. It is almost exactly the choice that Max Weber, founding figure of sociology, recommends to those considering the career of the scholar or the career of the politician: Carefully choose to be born into a family with money. In his essay "Politics as a Vocation," Weber famously distinguishes between living *for* and living *from* politics: "Those who make politics their permanent source of *income* are those who live 'from' the work of politics; those who do not are the ones who live 'for' politics."[2] In normal circumstances, he goes on, anyone who lives for politics will need to be "economically independent of any income politics may bring him. In simple terms: he needs to be rich." The work of politics cannot be done, or done properly, if the politician is not independent or, like an industrialist, is taken up with other kinds of business. By definition, then, "only private wealth can provide the necessary independence." The same holds for the would-be politician's availability: "The figure with the most such 'availability' is the rentier; in other words, someone who makes money without doing any work at all."

"Without doing any work at all"—for someone raised with a standard prejudice that under normal conditions income should be earned, this is a giveaway. It makes Weber sound more resigned than enthusiastic about his conclusion that the political leader needs to be rich, and indeed should be (as he was himself, through his wife) a rentier. Egalitarian objections are natural and inevitable. Will someone who is rich really tend to look out for the common good more than someone who is poor, or just not rich? And what about that independence? It's not hard to think of a recent American politician who has used his office to amass further wealth despite not absolutely needing to.

Weber includes scholars, like politicians, in the category of those requiring an inherited income. In Germany, he says, "only the rich can pursue an academic career . . . It is extraordinarily brave, not to say foolhardy, for an aspiring scholar who is not independently wealthy to confront the practical risks that go with an academic career." This you-have-to-be-rich logic casts an interesting light on the commitment to value-free autonomy that Weber did so much to bestow on present-day scholarship. Taking up for myself the cynical viewpoint of which I am elsewhere so suspicious, I speculate that scholarly autonomy might be understood as a laundered expression of the money behind it—that is, not so much value-free as bearing within itself an invisible deference to money and its value.

The speculation encourages us to follow the money. For example, what did Weber live on? After suffering a nervous breakdown, he gave up his academic post and lived for twenty intellectually fruitful years on an inheritance from his wife's family.[3] This much is well-known. But it is not customary to go beyond this biographical detail by asking: What inheritance? Where exactly did his wife's family money come from? To ask seems tactless, and maybe also pointless. What can one possibly learn from it? And yet answering the question of what Weber lived on turns up, to begin with, some intriguing information about his wife's family background. Guenther Roth's *Max Webers deutsch-englische Familiengeschichte, 1800–1950*, tells the story of the family money in detail. Weber's mother, Helene, was one of the daughters of Georg Friedrich Fallenstein and Emilie Souchay. Weber's maternal grandparents were rich. In Lutz Kaelber's words, "Financially, Georg Friedrich struck gold when he married Emilie Souchay, an heiress to the tremendous fortune accumulated by her father, Carl Cornelius Souchay."[4] Carl Cornelius, the great-grandfather on the mother's side, was a prototypical adventure capitalist whose activities included "speculation, carpet baggery, smuggling, and plain old savvy trading and finance . . . The family enterprise . . . included owning and operating a slave plantation in Cuba," and "Weber benefitted materially from being a member of a network of capitalists who had helped found and expand the first truly global and multi-ethnic form of capitalism." Weber's mother and her sisters were not the sole heirs of this fortune, but they were important beneficiaries of it.

The tension between Weber and his father that occasioned the nervous breakdown was as much monetary as psychological, and the money story goes back further. Weber's mother, like her sisters, "often had in mind more charitable purposes for their monies than their husbands, and on many occasions appear to have resented that their husbands' requests for an early and sometimes even increased distribution of their share in the inheritance be spent on material comforts." The father "had been unwilling to finance an independent household for his son, which meant that Weber Jr. was almost thirty when he was finally able to leave his parents' home for good." He thought he was entitled to independence on the basis of his mother's family money. But men had legal control over family finances, and the money was held back by his father. The 1897 encounter between father and son, which Roth calls "the family catastrophe," was precipitated by the father's treatment of the mother. Weber kicked his father out of his mother's house. Soon after, the father died. In the aftermath, Max had his nervous breakdown and began living on his wife's inheritance. Now, finally, he was financially independent.

The result of that independence was both a series of foundational works of independent-minded scholarship and an influential view of scholarship as itself independent. Did the source of the money have any impact on that result? It's hard to be sure, but it's not unlikely. Here is Kaelber again: "The fruits of his English-capitalist fathers' endeavors, the argument goes, allowed Weber to live the life of a scholar and *rentier*, and he expressed his gratitude to his late kin by sanitizing their economic actions and motives in his construction of ideal types of capitalism and projecting these actions and motives back onto a better, English past." To put this another way: "Weber was the scion of a newly emerged international bourgeoisie whose anglophile leanings led him to search for and find in the outlook of ideal-typical rational-methodical Britain businessmen of putative Puritan ancestry an imaginary liberal alternative to the authoritarian nationalism of imperial Germany." Weber brilliantly covered up the moral messiness of those enterprises in his groundbreaking scholarly treatment of capitalism's origins, *The Protestant Ethic and the Spirit of Capitalism*

(1904–5), a sociological account that distracted its readers from capitalism's antecedents in authoritarian nationalism, fraud, coercion, and plantation enslavement, which were also the antecedents of the fortune he personally lived on.

This story raises obvious questions about the doctrine of scholarly autonomy as well, which Weber tried to ground in the ideal of scholarship as value-free. Scholarship can arguably no more be free of value than it can be free of money. It is not free; it has to be paid for, and the money has to come from somewhere.

It does not follow that scholarly autonomy isn't worth defending. Today scholarly autonomy, such as it is, faces threats of political intervention unmatched since the reign of McCarthyism in the 1950s. But there are better and worse strategies for defending it. For those of us who want to defend in some degree the commitments to diversity, equity, and inclusion that are presently under government assault, for example, it is good to remember that not so long ago—in the 1970s and '80s—scholarly autonomy was invoked to keep such concerns *out* of higher education. It was pressure from outside the university that overcame that resistance and led to the institutional acceptance of such fields as women's studies and African-American studies—the field that taught scholars to look for things like the Cuban slave plantation and record its contribution to Weber's wife's inheritance. Most academics today are very glad those fields exist and for the moment are still funded. It would be inconsistent and indeed amnesiac for defenders of the university as it is to pretend that the university should not have to listen to voices from outside—or pay attention to the funding and investments that, like those voices, bind it causally to that outside. In the face of present threats that funding will be withdrawn, it's surely better, if also more challenging, to reconsider the dependence on that funding and what might be done with less of it. We can want to defend the university and want at the same time greater transparency about where and how the endowments, which sustain the autonomy of private universities, are invested. We ought to have a say as to whether endowments are invested in military contractors, say, who are facilitating and profiting from massacres.

I have been trying to suggest that following the money will not necessarily lead to an exposé. To repeat: There is no such thing as clean money. From this perspective, all we can look for is different kinds and degrees of dirt. To put this methodologically: There is no guarantee that following the money will lead to anything morally and politically comfortable.

That said, let us go down another monetary rabbit hole. In the introduction to her recent book-length revaluation of Weber, Wendy Brown notes that her volume is an expanded version of the Tanner Lectures on Human Values, presented at Yale University in 2019.[5] Brown adds that the Tanner Lectures are named for their "benefactor and founder, Obert Clark Tanner, a British Mormon philosopher, lawyer, theologian, industrialist, and philanthropist." For what it's worth, this list of professions is not in chronological order: O. C. Tanner was not born to wealth; he was first an industrialist who made a lot of money, and it was the money, of course, that allowed him to become a philanthropist. Burrowing once more, one discovers that Tanner started out manufacturing and selling class rings and pins. He then moved on, implausibly, to "employee recognition." Who would have imagined there was so much money to be made in the sale of "employee recognition awards"? The phrase makes you think of the proverbial gold watch at the end of the once-proverbial long work life in a single firm. (Tanner the brand also sold, and sells, gold watches.) The bitter taste left in the mouth by "employee recognition award" suggests the irony of long years on the job compensated not by commensurate salary or promotion to a position of decision-making, creativity, and responsibility, but by a symbolic and not very valuable trinket. There may be a faint poetic resonance here with Weber's linking of early capitalism with delayed gratification. The money for a lecture series on Weber comes from the mass production of trinkets awarded by the employer to the employee at the end of a perhaps overly faithful, perhaps overly self-denying work career.[6]

Having dug down so far, why not keep at it and dig a

little deeper? O.C. Tanner came into existence in 1927. As a high-end jeweler, selling rings and necklaces featuring diamonds, rubies, emeralds, and sapphires, among other precious stones, Tanner invites curiosity of the familiar "blood diamond" sort. In the 1920s and '30s, as the enterprise was taking off, the main source of its diamonds would presumably have been South Africa. There is no lack of books and films to satisfy those who might like to know more about the lives and deaths of the South Africans who did the diamond mining. Diamond mining in South Africa is usually dated to the discovery of alluvial diamonds in 1867. Moral concern on this topic already finds its way into the early pages of George Eliot's *Middlemarch* (1871–72).

It's always good to be reminded about the blood (the diamonds) and the boredom (the employee recognition rewards) out of which a philanthropy like this seems to have arisen. But is this information relevant in any significant way to the substance of Brown's lectures on "human values," her guarded but appreciative revaluation of Weber? Perhaps. The themes that seem most adventurous and unexpected in the Weber lectures, given Brown's strong radical bona fides, are leadership, responsibility, and nihilism. Weber's fear of radical mass movements led by demagogues made him "cultivate an ideal of leaders as *rulers,*" Brown writes, "and in turn to task rulers with the pursuit of a political vision, responsibly pursued." Here Brown shows some tolerance for the fact that "left-political mobilizations have become increasingly engaged by the question of leadership for large-scale transformations that exceed parliamentary tinkering but are short of revolution." Perhaps in reaction against the Democratic Party's misguided faith that an implacable demographic destiny is on its side, hence that it has no need for bold or visionary leadership, perhaps out of fear of populism, Brown takes a step away from radicalism, a step back in Weber's direction. Weber, as she reminds us, placed his hopes in a charismatic leader who, by definition, would not merely be the equal of his followers, or merely accountable to them after the fact. He would have to be responsible in a higher sense—responsible to the reality of their situation, which (as always) is a composite of diverse sufferings and injustices and must be miraculously synthesized and addressed in action that is effective and creative. Responsible for doing something.

Responsibility is a term that Brown, following Weber, repeats often. Her references in the Tanner lectures seem consistent with Antonio Y. Vázquez-Arroyo's argument in *Political Responsibility.* The usual invocations of responsibility, Vázquez-Arroyo suggests, are ethical; they neglect the inequalities of power in which all ethical acts take place. What the concept of responsibility needs is a politics, meaning a consciousness of acting in a situation of unequal power.[7] To say this, however, is not a mere gesture of political piety. It obliges us to take the risk of admitting that, in the struggle against unequal power, power is also something that must be acquired and exercised. That is the proposition I take Brown to be entertaining in Weber, at some peril to her moral or democratic principles, and yet in a way that furthers the creative project of democratic transformation. It seems possible that the financial support of the Tanner Lectures may have enabled this risk-taking. Some will imagine this hypothesis as the build-up to an eventual exposé that I am winding up to deliver. But there will be no exposé. Brown's insistence that the left needs to reconsider responsible leadership as an implicit alternative to abstract, leaderless egalitarianism seems to me worth the trouble she takes with it.

This is also a way of thinking about the privilege of the student protesters at Columbia—the privilege that enabled the student protesters to act. The students knew that they were not the ideal subjects of a revolutionary action. They had no confidence—that confidence would have been misplaced—that in the cold eyes of a sociologist they were properly placed so as to move history toward the justice they desired. They knew that, relatively speaking, even the less privileged among them were still privileged. What *were* they? Paul Berman imagined the protesters of 1968 as admitting, existentially, they were nothing and only came into being by what they did—as saying, "in effect: I struggle on behalf of others, therefore I am." The protesters of 2024 could have said much the same thing.[8]

As an interim conclusion, let me anticipate what I will want to argue again at the end. Under the present administration, we have excellent reasons to fear government scrutiny of how art, scholarship, and other cultural activities are funded. We have every reason to fear that funds will be cut or threatened for political reasons. Defunding has already happened, of course, and there seems to be more to come. And yet in the abstract, what we should want is, precisely, public scrutiny—public scrutiny of the funding of higher education, public scrutiny of the funding of cultural work in general, public decisions about where the money ought to go.

This proposal is very, very badly timed, I see that, the mood of the public being what it seems to be under the present administration and the notions of public service and public services having fallen into such ill repute. At this moment, public scrutiny can hardly mean anything but harsh, uncomprehending censorship and eventual defunding. And yet we have no choice but to hope that public scrutiny can and will be better educated—to hope, and to do the educational work needed make that change. To begin with, the general principle needs to be brought to the fore and the arguments made. As a smaller beginning, the professional arguers, people like ourselves, need to achieve greater clarity as to what we live on.

In *Poor Things: How Those with Money Depict Those without It* (2024), Lennard J. Davis cites Bourdieu to back up the contention "that writers who come from poverty . . . are essentially the only ones who have the platform and credentials to write about the poor."[9] This is the assumption on which slurs like "champagne socialist" and "limousine liberal" are based, though Davis, to his credit, allows the right to speak about poverty to those who are no longer poor as long as once upon a time they were. Other cultures pin the same charge of hypocrisy to other items of luxury consumption, like caviar in Spain and Portugal and chardonnay in Australia. Apparently "chardonnay socialist" went out of circulation in Australia when the country started to produce a lot of chardonnay and the vintage became widely available to the population at large. This is a possible model for the proper socialist position: There's nothing wrong with chardonnay as long as it's made widely available. Making good things like chardonnay or champagne widely available to the population at large is the goal.

Davis quotes Bourdieu: "Bourdieu, in his self-analysis, notes that he, coming from a lower-class background, could not do the kind of sociology that involves 'loftiness, a social distance, in which I could never feel at home and to which the relationship to the social world associated with certain social origins no doubt predisposes.'" Bourdieu is not wrong about the view of the world to which a prosperous upbringing predisposes. More of the people raised in households where champagne was routinely consumed probably ended up somewhere to the right of socialism.

More often than not, genuine privilege does not incline the genuinely privileged to reject the world that produced its privilege. William F. Buckley had less success with his fundraisers than Leonard Bernstein did. After failing to secure money to found *National Review*, he was obliged to take the funds from his father, who had made a fortune in oil in Mexico (where he worked well with a dictator) and Venezuela. In his outrage at Bernstein's support for the Panthers, Buckley is objecting to an exception, though not a rare one, to the causal chain that he himself exemplifies. That causality leads from extractive overseas fortunes like his father's to a life filled with servants, maids, and chauffeurs and onward to politics like those of *National Review*, which were to the right of Richard Nixon and Ronald Reagan. The personal qualifications Buckley could present to potential funders included a stint in the CIA, a book called *God and Man at Yale* (1951), which pioneered the right-wing attack on higher education (as atheistic), and support for the anti-Communist crusade of Joseph McCarthy. As mentioned above, it was on *National Review* that David Brooks began his journalistic career.[10]

Or take the example of The Free Press, founded by former *New York Times* opinion editor Bari Weiss. Weiss began her career as an undergraduate trying to get Columbia faculty members fired for pro-Palestinian views. That effort was funded and informed by the David Project, a pro-Israel campus group, itself funded by Combined Jewish Philanthropies (CJP), which funneled $1,514,942 from its donors to the organization between fiscal years 2007 and 2020. Additional funding came from organizations like the Joseph and Rae Gann Charitable Foundation, Kraft Family Philanthropies, and the Ruderman Family Foundation. The David Project was also supported by Seth Klarman and the Klarman Family Foundation. Information about the funding of The Free Press is freely available: Seed investors included venture capitalists Marc Andreessen, who worked with Elon Musk's DOGE, and Trump advisor David Sacks. Weiss herself comes from a family that owns or owned various New Jersey businesses, each with Weiss in its title. Nellie Bowles, also of The Free Press, spouse of Weiss, and notorious for her lack of sympathy for protesters, is a self-described debutante. According to Wikipedia, she is also a descendant of Henry Miller, who was dubbed the "Cattle King of California" and was at one point one of the largest landowners in the United States.[11] She is also a descendant of Thomas Crowley, who founded the transportation and logistics company Crowley Maritime, with a fleet of more than three hundred vessels.[12]

This is what Bourdieu calls the way of the world. Luckily, it is not the absolute rule. The Gaza protesters are one exception to it.

An inheritance comes from a family, as Weber's did. Someone in your family might leave you money because they love you, however you have behaved or misbehaved in the past. Society, on the other hand, is not a family. Society does not fund you because it loves you. And you may not love society back. Indeed, as an intellectual or artist or other cultural worker, you may well define what you do as in some way standing against or apart from society—as misbehaving. How is it, then, that society will agree to pay, to the extent that it does, to sustain the life of those who contest society, if only minimally? How is it that, in paying its adversaries, society may even nurture some of them to the point where they can be described as privileged?[13]

There are two main reasons why people want to read about intellectuals. One is that they are famous and admired, like Susan Sontag. The second is that they got famous and admired by *being* dissenters, or at least *while* being dissenters. Practically speaking, the issue is not so much that intellectuals or student demonstrators or other examples of the cultural elite are privileged, that they have too much money. The deeper irritation is that society is willing to pay them *anything at all*, given that their goal is—if indeed it is—the criticism of society. There is a paradox here: Dissent or complaint or rebellion comes with a certain authority. It is *authorized* or even *empowered* dissent.

One traditional way to think of this paradox is to consider that intellectuals, like writers and artists, stand in for what in a more religious society would once have been called the sacred. If intellectuals are indeed a secularized vestige of the sacred, as Julien Benda suggested in *La Tra-*

hison des clercs (1927), if the expectation continues to be that they represent some version of transcendence, something higher than the reproduction of biological life, something higher than the ordinary struggle to make ends meet, then disappointment would be a perpetual possibility, even an inevitability: disappointment that the representatives of the immaterial turn out to be as material in their demands of life as everyone else, to be as concerned with creature comforts, or to be concerned with making a living at all. This hypothesis, which comes in more and less politicized versions, would help explain why intellectuals are so often accused of betraying, absconding, disappearing, being academicized or (to come back to earning a living) bourgeoisified. In the good old days, it is said, intellectuals were properly independent, properly detached. Now they have jobs like everyone else. "The relative decline of unattached intellectuals over the last thirty or forty years," Lewis Coser writes, ". . . is part of the growing institutionalization and, more particularly, academization of intellect in America."[14] "Men like Edmund Wilson, who has consistently refused such attachment, have come to look like monuments of a half-forgotten past."

Any way of making a living, any social embodiment, is a sign that the species has gone extinct. This cliché was so pervasive in the culture wars that I found myself calling it out in 1990: "Obituaries for the intellectual . . . are so per-sistent a genre because intellectuals have never lived the gloriously independent life so often ascribed to them, and thus must always appear, when observed closely, to be on the point of losing it."[15] Claiming that we have seen the last of the intellectuals is of course a way of celebrating them as an ideal. But it also feeds into a willed blindness as to the actual funds behind so-called independence—to take relevant examples, New York intellectuals marrying women with money or selling their wares on the journalistic market, perhaps even to Condé Nast. Selling your writing on the journalistic market is not a moral sin, but neither is it properly described as independence, as anyone can tell you who has done it. Depending on the market is also dependence. And where did the wives get that money? The narrative of bourgeoisification sounds like it would sustain a politics of equality. But it nurtures a demonetized anti-elitism. It's as if intellectuals really ought to starve. Starving is not an option. Dissent is socially necessary. And dissent has to be located *somewhere.*

The paradox of dissent that is gainfully employed, and to that extent at least also empowered, helps explain the ambivalence that trips lightly through the pages of *What Was the Hipster? A Sociological Investigation*, a volume published by the editors of the journal *n+1*.[16] The volume does not declare that hipsters have trust funds. But it acknowledges again and again that there are financial resources, almost certainly unearned, behind style statements that rival in ostentation Nerval's strolling through Paris with a lobster on a leash, and the point seems to be that inherited money makes possible this proudly unproductive neo-bohemian lifestyle, which remains merely wishfully adversarial. Why, then, pick such a subject? As Mark Greif writes in his introduction to the book, "The topic seems too stupid and demeaning . . . The hipster represents, in a deep way, a tendency we founded the journal to combat; yet he exists on our ground, in our neighborhood and particular world, and is an intimate enemy—also a danger and temptation." Greif might have added that a self-distancing attack on the hipster came out in issue three. He does say that both *n+1*'s neighborhood and the hipster style are recognizably bohemian, in the line of Bourdieu's nineteenth-century Paris, and he strongly recommends the reading of Bourdieu's *Distinction* for anyone taking on the topic.[17]

Yet the volume contains little to no celebration of the hipster. On the contrary, its summary judgments of the hipster are not magnanimous:

> The hipster represents what can happen to middle-class whites, particularly, and to all elites, generally, when they focus on the struggles for their own pleasures and luxuries—seeing these as daring and confrontational—rather than asking what makes their sort of people entitled to them, who else suffers

> for their pleasures, and where their 'rebellion' adjoins social struggles that should obligate anybody who hates authority.

And again: "Hipster anti-authoritarianism bespeaks a ruse by which the middle-class young can forgive themselves for abandoning the claims of counterculture—whether punk, anti-capitalist, anarchist, nerdy, or 60s—while retaining the coolness of subculture." Ungenerous judgments may be in order, but the reason for them advanced here is not, as one might have expected, that hipster oppositionality is merely symbolic and shouldn't count as real politics. It's that hipsters have money. They have money, and that is why daring to present themselves to the world as oppositional is embarrassing and unacceptable.

On closer examination, however, the volume is not completely certain that hipsters *do* have money, at least in the strong sense. Christian Lorentzen claims, perhaps tongue in cheek, "that hipsters exist in a state of perpetual luxuriant slumming and that rich people and people who grew up poor colluded in a group project of class confusion, conspiring to blur class boundaries temporarily in order to allow themselves to socialize and sleep with each other." If hipsters are "slumming," they are unquestionably from the dominant class. On the other hand, Greif writes: "The hipster is that person, overlapping with declassing or disaffiliating groupings—the starving artist, the starving graduate student, the neo-bohemian, the vegan or bicyclist or skate punk, the would-be blue-collar or post-racial individual—who in fact aligns himself *both* with rebel subculture *and* with the dominant class, and opens up a poisonous conduit between the two." Leaving "poisonous" aside, to say that the hipster "aligns himself" with the dominant class is not to say that the hipster actually *comes from* the dominant class. It's not to say, for example, that the hipster has a trust fund. Greif leaves open the possibility that some hipsters are not trust fund intellectuals at all, but perhaps (to keep to the symmetry) food stamp intellectuals.[18]

A few pages later, Lorentzen writes, "I meanwhile continued to be broke. I haven't bought any new clothes since 2005." His essay ends: "My advice is to stay out of debt." This is comic, but debt may be as relevant to the financial description of the hipster as either food stamps or trust funds. Credit card debt, which as a massive phenomenon is relatively recent, has created a zone between having and not having money that makes certain styles of life possible, if only until the credit card bills have to be paid. It's true, as Jace Clayton writes, that "trying to live cheaply doesn't make you working class." But perhaps some hipsters could, in fact, be described as working class. From another perspective, it is conceivable that for many who might be called hipsters, the category is just a way of dressing up as positively as the circumstances permit a genuine lack of money, which is to say an apartment with bedbugs and roommates and a job as a waiter, allow. Another contributor speaks of WASHes, or Waitstaff and Service Hipsters.[19] The hipster's conspicuous identification with "white trash," conveyed through trucker hats, wife beaters, and lumberjack flannels, sends us back to the Democratic Party's lost white manual-labor constituency. The gesture is helplessly open to ridicule, but its "shouldn't we be thinking of that constituency?" impulse is not totally incoherent or grossly misguided. Or maybe it should be "are we sure that's not who we are?"[20]

Political opinions, artistic stances, can't live on air. They need some sort of funding. If Nerval was indeed in pursuit of a stable, secure income, I for one do not lose all respect for him.

Origin stories are notoriously unreliable. Nations rarely come into existence without some more or less unpalatable violence that the official narrative will later cover up.[21] Consider from this angle the little magazines, indispensable locus of bohemian, countercultural existence. What do little magazines live on? Although they may not be intended to turn a profit, with respect to origin stories little magazines are no different from nations or larger magazines, and there is something to be learned from what their origin stories do and don't say about the creative leadership that enabled their creation.

Of the founding of *n+1*, the journal that hosted the conversation about the hipster, Mark Greif, one of the original editors, writes:

> We were very proud that we were able to start it without outside funds, and really on a shoestring . . . four of us put in $2000 each, and we vowed to sell one hundred subscriptions, each for $20 (I think that's right), from the "sample"/prototype issue. We were able to sell out the copies of the first printed issue, letting us fund number two; subscriptions expanded when it got written about in the NYT; people started to donate; we went along that way till interns started to help/work so much that they needed to be paid. After a few years there was a big question of whether to become a nonprofit/public charity, and we did so. Till a couple of years ago the budget was paid in about an equal split between subscription revenues and fundraising (donations, grants, gala dinner); I think in the last few years things have started to tilt toward fundraising, and also our budget, which used to run big surpluses (lots of free labor, and low costs), has been running steady deficits, as the payroll costs on real jobs (including health care) stay and grow and as our subs don't really climb significantly . . . But that is its own saga.[22]

This is a lovely origin story. The pride seems entirely justified. Narratively speaking, of course, this story invites a deflating contrast between the self-funded purity of the origin and the subsequent "tilt toward fundraising." But fundraising is not mortally sinful, and it also helps to recall that origins are never entirely pure. To say that, like Leavis's *Scrutiny*, *n+1* was totally self-funded at the outset and was staffed by volunteers is to say, among other things, that the editors had at least some disposable income or savings, however meager, and that they and the other volunteers presumably had some other means of keeping themselves alive.[23] This does not make the enterprise elite in the monetary sense, despite the founding editors' prestigious and expensive educations. It means only that the pretense of absolute pennilessness is disallowed and that it matters to the narrative; it makes up the narrative middle, which is as important as the beginning—how the pennies are disbursed. Keith Gessen, another of the founders, writes:

> That first real office was a great advance for us; so was our first office manager, Isaac Scarborough, who worked for free in exchange for getting to sit in the office and do his other (paid) work there. In 2006, Isaac went off to the Peace Corps in Turkmenistan, but we were able to hire our best intern, Alexandra (Ali) Heifetz, to a barely livable wage as our business manager. Ali heroically remained on the job for as long as she could, doing everything—subscription fulfillment, accounting, distribution, layout—in that dark office, until she could take it no more and went off to law school. It wasn't until 2010 that we were able to hire a second full-time employee, so that we had both a

> business manager and a managing editor. As of this writing, we're at three and a half full-time employees, which seems about right. Aside from a few months over the past decade when a few of us were too impoverished to carry out our magazine duties (running production, in one case; overseeing the office, in another) and asked for a stipend, none of the founding editors has been paid.

Is it of any moral significance that, since that origin, *n+1* (along with such progressive magazines as *The Baffler*, *Jewish Currents*, *Lux*, and *Dissent*) has also received funding from George Soros's Open Society Foundation? There is no doubt much to be said about where and how George Soros made the money that he has been giving away so generously, but the right cannot say it, since worse things would also have to be said about its own funders. Hence they prefer antisemitic allusions.

The story about the founding of *Dissent* that its editors tell is similar. A conference was announced in 1954. Lewis Coser writes: "The response was heartening. If memory serves me right, there were some 50 people at the conference, practically all of whom promised to contribute articles or money, preferably both" ("The First 25 Years").[24] But there is another story behind this origin. The story the editors don't tell is how much of *Dissent*'s early funding was provided by Joseph Buttinger, who was involved with the

CIA, though he began life as a socialist in Austria. Later, Buttinger was a defender of the war in Vietnam.[25]

Monthly Review had the good fortune to be funded by a gift from F.O. Mathiessen, a titan of American literary studies and closeted socialist who committed suicide when he feared he would be outed by McCarthy's House Committee on Un-American Activities. Mathiessen had inherited the money ($15,000 in the late 1940s, about $200,000 today) from his grandfather. His grandfather started as a manufacturer of zinc, which turned out to be crucial to the arms industry. The arms industry, like the weapons manufacturers in which Columbia University's endowment is invested, will not stand as the platonic ideal of magazine funding.[26] On the other hand, the case can be made that at that moment the arms industry was supplying the Union army during the Civil War, which is arguably as close to a good war as the U.S. has fought.

A new funding source was needed when *Partisan Review* broke with the Communist Party in 1937 and was reborn as an organ of the anti-Stalinist left. In Terry Cooney's history of the journal, that source is named as George L.K. Morris. Cooney presents Morris as a painter friend of Dwight Macdonald, a painter who "had the means to finance PR."[27] Delving a little deeper, one finds that Morris's family had had the means for generations. His paternal grandfather, descended from a signer of the Declaration of Independence, was already wealthy enough to be considered "a man of leisure." Wikipedia informs us that "He was a governor, and one of the founders, of the Metropolitan Club, a member of the Union Club of New York, member of the New York Young Republican Club, president of the Suburban Riding and Driving Club, president of the Ridgefield Club, a director of the Coney Island Jockey Club, a director of the National Horse Show Association, a member of the Riding Club, the Automobile Club, and the Delta Phi fraternity." It does not inform us that he was also on the Board of Trustees of Columbia University. More recently, Columbia's trustees distinguished themselves during the Gaza massacre by enthusiastically embracing the Republican Party's call for a crackdown on the Gaza protesters.

One does not have to dig deep at all, thanks to the work of Stonor Saunders and others, to be reminded of the jaw-dropping role played by the Central Intelligence Agency in getting and keeping *Partisan Review* above water, for example by solving its problems with the Internal Revenue Service.[28] It is the CIA, not the IRS, that gets all the attention in this narrative twist, and rightly so. The IRS, a branch of the Department of the Treasury, may seem peripheral to the topic of what intellectuals live on. But the more one looks, the more attention is drawn toward taxes, which Edmund Wilson hated enough to write an entire book about them. Take taxes away or cut them to the bone, a program that is of course quite active in our time, and where would public funding for public services be? The National Endowment for the Humanities, which supported Cooney's research, is (or perhaps I should say was, given the dismantling of the federal bureaucracy) a federal agency. This is a period when the people who inhabit the world of trust funds, whether they receive, bestow, or manage those funds, have been trying to defund the Supplemental Nutrition Assistance Program, or SNAP, meaning food stamps, and the intellectuals who depend on food stamps rather than trust funds. In such a period, it is important to note in passing that Cooney is thanking the state. For all its many sins, the state deserves his thanks, and the thanks of many others.[29]

How *do* little magazines manage to pay their writers, editors, and fact-checkers the pittance those essential cultural workers try to live on? The first answer that comes to mind is probably not taxes. And yet taxes, or the support of the state, is a motif that can be traced through a number of periodical biographies, sometimes in unexpected ways. In 1992, there was a reboot of the *New Left Review* in which, according to Duncan Thompson's history of the journal[30], a "sharp dispute over ownership and control of the journal" was resolved "by recourse to the legal owners of the journal, the shareholders." Shares and ownership were now "vested in a new Trust, trustees comprising Perry Anderson, his brother Benedict, both now based in North America, and Ronald Fraser, who had resigned from the review in 1977 and was now living in Spain." According to a letter to "Contributors and Friends" circulated by editor Robin Blackburn on March 19, 1993, Perry Anderson, Benedict Anderson, and Ronald Fraser had been the "three donors who had put the review's finances on a sound footing in the sixties." It seems the money was very likely decisive.[31] Where did the money come from? For the Anderson brothers, land in Ireland is no doubt somewhere in the background, perhaps far enough back so that nothing need be said about British colonialism. Closer to the foreground, the father of Perry and Benedict Anderson worked for the Chinese Maritime Customs Service (CMCS). This is the account of the CMCS given in Benedict Anderson's memoir:

> Originally set up by the British and French imperialists, it was designed to make sure the Ch'ing dynasty paid the huge indemnities imposed on it after the "successful" assault on Peking in 1860 during the Second Opium War. In effect it took control over the taxation of China's maritime trade with the outside world.

Anderson adds that its outlook gradually changed, "so that it increasingly tried to serve what it saw as China's real interests, especially after the fall of the Ch'ing dynasty in 1911 and the onset of the age of the warlords."[32]

Anderson's memoir does not say that his father and the CMCS enriched themselves at the expense of the Chinese people, as one might have expected from the institution's imperial origins, and, for that matter, the tradition of writers and intellectuals whose fathers had made a personal fortune as so-called tax farmers. It seems quite likely that, implausible as it might seem, the CMCS acted like a state in the absence of a state—acted like a state in the least objectionable sense. If so, nothing conclusively damaging can be said about the presumably inherited tax-related money that enabled a change of personnel at *New Left Review* in 1992–3 and prevented a hypothetical change in editorial direction, however one might feel about either.

After its entirely self-funded origin, *n+1* came to receive substantial funding from New York State. Those figures are public.[33] It too received a grant from the National Endowment for the Arts, or the federal government—a grant that disappeared with Trump's second term. But before the public funding became available, the editors discovered that the state could provide game-changing support in quieter ways: "We'd take a backpack to the post office for regular mailings, and for the big issue mailing at the start of the cycle we'd borrow a car. Then someone—it must have been Ali Heifetz, our first full-time managing editor—discovered that the post office will actually come and pick up your mail at your office if you ask them to. Nothing was ever the same after that."[34] Gessen is exaggerating for comic effect, but it's not an exaggeration to say that when public funds and public services are factored in, nothing about the "what did X live on?" question is the same. If you work for the post office (even if the post office is no longer entirely public), you are serving the common good, and the survival of $n+1$ is part of the common good.

The purpose behind the forming of a new, meritocratic elite, as Nicholas Lemann observes, was "administrative and scholarly service to a modern bureaucratic state." Like so many allusions to elites, their intended service to the modern bureaucratic state is often assumed to serve sinister purposes, beginning with Weber's narrative of fatal bureaucratic rationalization. It was the rise of a new bureaucracy, as Weber saw, that brought new sociological attention to the concept. But it did not follow, as some feared, that the elite that staffed the bureaucracy was now the real power behind the sham power of the government. Civil service jobs—in Weber's time, that included scholars—were located in Weber's eyes within rationality's iron cage, to be sure, but the value of that sometimes callous and unjust rationality must be weighed against both the anarchic counter-rationality of the profit motive and the arbitrary whims of charismatic authoritarians like the ones who have recently been trying to destroy state agencies and fire their employees.

In *Men of Ideas: A Sociologist's View,* Coser, cofounder of *Dissent,* quotes Weber's formula about living either for or from politics in order to suggest that intellectuals, too, should properly be detached from ordinary worries about earning a living: "Intellectuals live for rather than from ideas."[35] That said, Coser also notes that intellectuals are in fact earning a living now (like the majority of observers, he fails to mention how the "unattached" intellectuals earned a living before). They are doing so by working both in academia and in the institutions of the welfare state. The post office offers a fresh and useful perspective on this welfare state twist in the narrative of intellectuals. In her history of *Dissent*, Bulik notes that in the same years in which the journal "began to take on a more scholarly tone," it also shifted in topic, until, by the end of the seventies, "*Dissent* could have been subtitled 'discussions on the welfare state.'" If so, this would be evidence of the journal's analytic perspective and choice of themes aligning with its economic means, or vice versa. Is there anything to deplore or even regret here? Writers for *Dissent* were recognizing, however indirectly, that intellectuals can and perhaps must depend for their livelihood on public funds, democratically decided upon. Morally speaking, that dependence can be freely admitted. It's not a shameful way to earn a living. Of course, that's not the way everyone sees it.

During the last set of culture wars, in the 1980s and 1990s, it was often suggested that there was an unholy alliance between intellectuals of the left and the racial, ethnic, and sexual minorities in whose name the intellectuals often purport to speak. The alliance was assumed to be unholy because those same intellectuals hoped to earn a living by offering services to people in need, and those people in need were paradigmatically members of minorities. The charge was that the welfare state offers undeserved welfare for the bureaucrats who serve it as well as for those it serves.[36] It seems possible to admit that charge provisionally, disputing only the implication that the services, if rendered, must be unreal or useless or wrongheaded and thus that the bureaucrats' income is somehow unearned, parasitic, not a wage but a privilege.

And in today's culture wars, again this should be no surprise, merely desiring a steady job with an income and benefits has again become an accusation.[37] It seems likely that the student protesters who are accused of wanting jobs were and are eager to do something socially meaningful, in their demonstrations and (if possible) also in their jobs. The possibility of doing something meaningful *in your job*, something that aims at the common good rather than at a company's balance sheet and an employee recognition reward at the end of long years of faithful labor, something that is self-interested but at the same in the public interest, arises when state agencies are delegated to offer public services, whether in the form of picking up a journal's mail at its office or in more dramatic governmental activities like inspecting the purity of food, air, and water, testing the safety of medicines, regulating toxic dumping, ensuring safe working conditions, protecting consumers from fraud, and keeping airplanes from colliding with each other.

All these activities are in the public eye these days because they, like universities, are being aggressively attacked and dismantled. None of the agencies that do this work is an ideal version of itself, but they do not (as is claimed about universities) merely seek to reproduce an unbearable status quo. In any event, like universities, and for that matter like little magazines, they receive society's money. In other words, they depend on taxes, and on the belief in taxes. There are good reasons for disbelief in taxes—for example, the inequality with which taxes are ingeniously exacted and avoided, and of course their military uses.[38] But there are also bad reasons. In this context, what matters is that belief in taxes has been undermined by the channeling of legitimate popular discontent into anti-statism and anti-elitism.

FOUR

BOURDIEU AND TAXES

As it happens, Bourdieu had a chance to rethink his position. His *Free Exchange* (1995) is a book of dialogues published in collaboration with the German conceptual artist Hans Haacke, whose work had been influenced by Bourdieu. In a long artistic career, Haacke had already devoted a great deal of attention to the discovery of where the money for art comes from, and naturally enough the dialogues between the two often turned on that subject. Haacke's work, like Bourdieu's, is confrontational; much of it would count as exposé. But his position on elite experts is not a radical egalitarian one. There is a place on the left for experts and managers: "No organization, certainly not a complex society like ours, can survive without managers. I am sure we gain by the presence of intellectuals in managerial positions."

Perhaps in the spirit of the exchange, Bourdieu too recognizes that his own egalitarian sociology is bound to existing social inequality. For example, the unequal distribution of money: "One of the problems for the social sciences is obtaining the resources necessary to research (sociology is expensive)." Bourdieu is clearly uneasy with this situation. What does it mean for him to depend on funding from the state? What does he think of management as something states do? Look at the two sentences that precede this one: "All authoritarian regimes have suppressed sociology from the outset. What they want is an applied sociology that can help them manage conflicts and contradictions and rationalize domination." These sentences expose a world of contradiction. Authoritarian regimes want to suppress sociology. But no, a certain sociology (he calls it "applied") is useful to authoritarian regimes because it helps them manage conflicts and so on. How can Bourdieu be sure that his own sociology is not similarly "applied," is not similarly serving to help "manage conflicts and contradictions?" Without noticing the trap he has set for himself, Bourdieu skips blithely away. Suddenly, he presents sociology as whole again, back to being what authoritarian regimes (unlike the regime in France) want to suppress. Now, as a whole discipline, it has the problem of raising money. Presumably from the state. Bourdieu must be assuming that France, which gives him money and supports a sociology that is not "applied," not aimed at managing conflicts and contradictions, is not an authoritarian state. If his sociology does not do those things, then its funder must approve. But that would suggest a portrait of the French state that Bourdieu clearly does not want to embrace; praise of the French state as nonauthoritarian is not high on Bourdieu's agenda. But at this moment in history, the only resolution of Bourdieu's dilemma—which is not his alone—is funding approved by a state that is at least minimally democratic, at least minimally committed to the welfare of its citizens.

To judge from its opening pages, the occasion for the collaboration on *Free Exchange* was the American controversy over supposedly sacrilegious and pornographic art—Andres Serrano's *Piss Christ* and the photographs of Robert Mapplethorpe. Both had been funded by the National Endowment for the Humanities (NEH), that is, by the American state. The charge was that "public funds had been used to subsidize a sacrilege." In defending the public funding of controversial art, Haacke is quietly offering Bourdieu an answer to the funding dilemma he lays out for sociology. And Haacke underlines this answer by mentioning that, in the resulting trial, the jury unexpectedly found the museum director not guilty and did so on the grounds that, whatever they thought themselves, the experts said this really was art. Respect for expertise, respect for the state's willingness to claim expertise and engage in self-conscious artistic sponsorship: These were not to be taken for granted then, and there is less reason to rely on them now. But what better answers do we have to the question of what to live on?

The terms in which Haacke defends public funding reflect critically on Bourdieu's cynical sociology. "These events have taught artists and intellectuals that, aside from individual success in terms of money and fame, there are other things that matter," he writes. The lessons learned, in Haacke's view, are antithetical to cynicism.

The occasion seems to have invited Bourdieu to reflect further on how his own work has been funded. He initially strikes a defensive note: "When I wanted to undertake a study of photography, I accepted support from Kodak, not so much for the money, which was an insignificant amount, but rather for information, especially statistics, that only the company could provide." Accepting Kodak's support got him "extraordinary reprobation," he adds, responding that the reprobation would have been justified if the resulting book had carried "the Kodak trademark." Does funding leave a trademark, or some other mark? Haacke enters into the issue with a certain indirection. He cites the opinion of Hilton Kramer, editor of the *New Criterion*, that those "hostile to the policies of the US government" do not deserve government grants. Kramer, a traditionalist, does not demand that art be aligned with government policy; that would be the totalitarian, not the free-world, view. Kramer holds that art should be politically independent. As he tells the story, the villain is politics. The "'radical movements of the Sixties' . . . have destroyed 'the very notion of an independent high culture." Two pages earlier, however, Haacke has offered evidence that Kramer's independent high culture is a figment of Kramer's imagination. How is the *New Criterion* itself funded? "Like other journals of the network, [the *New Criterion*] is subsidized by the 'four sisters' [that is, the Sarah Scaife, John M. Olin, Smith Richardson, and Lynde and Harry Bradley foundations, all of them supporting right-wing organizations]. Since its founding in 1982, until 1990, it received $2.5 million. Its most faithful sponsor is the John M. Olin Foundation in New York. Every year it gives $100,000 . . . The Olin Foundation ranks among the big American producers of ammunition, including poison gas. William Simon, the president of the Foundation, went around collecting money for the Contras, as did Elliott Abrams."[1] Militarism, as the ultimate source of Kramer's funding, successfully disguises itself as "independent high culture" until (Haacke modestly does not say this) Haacke himself digs down and uncovers it.

Writers and artists, Bourdieu writes, are "quite often not aware that they have common interests." If this is true, as Haacke also suggests, Bourdieu must take some of the blame for it. Throughout his career, and especially in the account of bohemian Paris, he insisted that writers and artists were motivated by individual self-interest, whether in the form of status or in a form of status eventually convertible into money. And yet whether because of the gravitational pull of being in extended dialogue with Haacke, or his own late desire to play the role of public intellectual, here he stresses the need to think in terms of *common* interests. He also accepts something more important. An agent was required that could allow sociology to represent the common interest, and could allow it to be funded as such, and that agent has been the French state. Affirming the need for the state to fund public culture, he freely admits that this has been true for him, as it has for Haacke: "If, for example, I had to find sponsors to finance my research, I would have a hard time. As would you." It's the paradox of empowered dissent: "Culture with a critical perspective . . . can only be assured by the state."

How bad should Bourdieu feel about being funded by a state that, in France as in the US, is always ready to reveal the hidden face of military violence? In search of an answer, I beg you to follow me, kind reader, as I go down one last rabbit hole. The publisher's note to *Free Exchange*, inscribed across from the title page, informs the reader that the discussions and research that went into the book were "initiated by the Fondation de France." What, you ask, is the Fondation de France, which not merely funded this project but also initiated it? The Fondation de France presents itself as a private establishment of public utility, founded by the French government in 1969 to stimulate and foster the growth of private philanthropy.[2] It's clear that in order to bring it into existence, much initial skepticism had to be overcome, and not just by the big banks that were asked for initial donations.

In 1966, a fact-finding mission to the United States, land of foundations, came back confirming Max Weber's comparison between the abundance of private foundations in Protestant America as opposed to their scarcity in Catholic, centralized France, where humanitarianism tended to be public, managed by the state, and funded by taxation. The idea was that the Fondation de France would help the country trace for itself a "third path," neither free in the capitalist sense nor authoritarian in the Communist tradition. Still, there was resistance. Why did the French state, in the person of Charles de Gaulle, finally decide to sign on? By now it was 1969. In part, it seems, de Gaulle wanted to head off further "troubles" of the sort French society had just seen in 1968. It was also in the aftermath of the student (and worker) disruptions of May that Sartre decided to fund *Libération*. You might say that it was the social energies of 1968, which seemed to Hilton Kramer to have destroyed the very notion of high independent art, that encouraged the French state to step in. The state was pushed from below, and that is how it ended up both funding and initiating a project like the dialogue of Bourdieu and Haacke. A subversive project that has surely inspired many to indulge their curiosity about where the money for artists and writers comes from. But also—and maybe this is the mark or trademark of the funding that *Free Exchange* received—a project that is not cynical about what its authors live on.

Three years before his death, Gérard de Nerval published a biographical study of six eccentrics. The need for money was clearly one motive; he had published all of this material before. One of his subjects was Nicolas Restif de la Bretonne

(1734–1806), a novelist and utopian who had imagined, as Nerval says, a local association of workers and tradesmen who would exchange goods and services only with each other and thus would have no need of money.[3] Restif de la Bretonne was himself in great need of money. But in his account of the eighteenth-century writer's death, Nerval anticipates what the author of *De Quoi Vivait Gérard de Nerval* would say about his own: "On dit à tort que Restif était mort dans la misère." It's wrong to say that Restif died in poverty. Restif lost his savings with the fall of the *assignats*, a monetary instrument that had been invented during the Revolution and had depreciated quickly and dramatically. But he was saved from destitution, Nerval goes on, by the French state. His friends managed to get him a state subsidy.

EPILOGUE

There is no documentary evidence that Gérard de Nerval took an active role, or any role at all, in the Revolution of 1848. He had sympathies with the revolutionary cause, but he was preoccupied with writing and publishing. I have at least this much in common with Nerval: In the student protests of the late 1960s, I too played no active role. On May 9, 1970, I did not join the student uprising at Harvard that had brought buses filled with police to Harvard Square, marching in formation and chanting "God Bless America." I was getting married that day. I was thinking about love, not activism.

In the fall of 1968, my elementary French class had been presented with some of the slogans from the events of the Paris springtime. *Sous les pavés, la plage. Nous sommes tous indésirables. Il est interdit d'interdire. Cours, camarade, le vieux monde est derrière toi!* You didn't have to know much French to see that these were cool lines. But I didn't get much closer than that to the world-shaking coolness of the sixties. I was as far behind my classmates politically as intellectually. I had to catch up. I had homework to do. Someone else thought up the slogans and made the banners, and I marched behind them. Or, if I didn't feel I had time, I didn't. When the SDS organized an occupation of the administration building in 1969, my former roommate (I had moved in with my beloved; perhaps not a smart move, in retrospect) was with the crowd on the grass out in front. The police had sealed off the area. I arranged to meet him at a dark corner of the fence and slip him a bottle of wine and a blanket. Then I ran off to see my beloved. When heads were beaten and arrests were made, I was elsewhere.

Another day, my beloved and I were forced off the pavement by a phalanx of heavily armored cops, marching to clear the streets of protestors. But we weren't arrested, and on May 9, 1970, after the big march (the press called it a riot, and Clarence Thomas credits it with turning him off the left), while Cambodia was being bombed by B-52s and those hard-hatted construction workers were beating up on anti-war protesters in New York, we had our little wedding. On its way to the university room we had reserved for our festivities, the wedding party briefly stopped traffic. It was shameless jaywalking. It probably raised some eyebrows. But it wasn't the revolution.

Fifty-five years later, in the spring of 2025, I was notified by the Office of Institutional Equity at Columbia University that there was a "finding" in my case. The case had been brought against me by two anonymous students a year before. On April 22, 2024, there was an encampment protesting the atrocities currently being committed in Gaza. The course I was teaching was about atrocity, and since January the syllabus for that week had specified "Gaza, readings to be announced." I had invited the class to propose readings and had put all the readings proposed onto the website. Then, on the morning of April 22, the encampment appeared, steps away from our classroom, and in my opinion the class had a historic opportunity: the opportunity to discuss atrocity in Gaza in the presence of their fellow students, who were taking action against those atrocities. I told the class I personally wanted to take advantage of this opportunity, but anyone who was not comfortable coming to the encampment should not come; of course, there would be no penalty for not coming. The administration's announcement expressed concern for the safety of the students and advised offering the option of holding class virtually, but it did not close the campus off, and no one in my class asked for class to be held virtually. Having seen how peaceful the demonstrations were, I did not fear for anyone's safety. There was no reason to. Those students who wanted to come along came. It was quiet and peaceful. There was no hint of antisemitism. (As everyone hopefully knows by now, a Passover seder was held on the encampment.) I made a little speech to my students about how complicated it was to judge atrocities; my example was my father's service as a bomber pilot in World War II, when he fought Nazism (which was a good thing to do) but also killed civilians on the ground, which now had to count as an atrocity. Two of the students who didn't come brought charges.

The university took those charges seriously. It found me guilty of discrimination and harassment. It said I had violated the students' right to equality of educational opportunity on the basis of their national identity. It seems that, according to the university's interpretation of Title VI of the 1964 Civil Rights Act, which is the Trump administration's interpretation, any criticism of the Israeli military amounts to criticism of Israel itself, and since military conscription is universal in Israel, that is equivalent to criticism of national identity, or antisemitism (a word that the lawyer who "trained" me never pronounced. My "training" was a conversation that lasted about an hour and a half. There was a certain amount of laughter). Perhaps because I am Jewish, they didn't try to get me to retire, as they did a colleague in the Law School. The training was just a slap on the wrist. I didn't say that by the lawyer's criteria, conscription also being universal in Nazi Germany, criticism of the conduct of the Nazi military would also have been a violation of the Civil Rights Act. I didn't reveal that a journalist had filmed my little speech at the encampment, showing pretty clearly (if anyone cared) that what had happened there was not propaganda, but a genuinely educational moment. I had been advised that if I showed the footage, I might be putting in danger students whose faces appeared in it.

The student protesters, whether they were arrested and

suspended or not, already risked losing a great deal. Many were doxed (trucks circled the Columbia campus advertising their names), and some had offers of employment in law firms rescinded. We will probably never know how far and how wide the Zionist blacklist extends. For many of the bravest, it will be much harder to find a decent job. Foreign students were threatened with deportation for doing nothing more than exercising their free speech rights. Many of them risked more of their futures than their American fellow students could imagine. And yet all of them can be considered privileged. They are privileged in the sense that, being at Columbia, they already knew better than most people how to gather and evaluate relevant information and, having puts the facts together, how to make their voices heard. This is what Chomsky called, in the era of resistance to the war in Vietnam, the "responsibility of intellectuals."[1] Arguably there is no responsibility that is not grounded in some degree of privilege. There is a privilege, and a responsibility, that comes merely with being dispensed, at least temporarily, from the necessity of making a living.

It seems unlikely, the political situation being what it is, that society will decide any time soon to extend this privilege to more people and more institutions. But many of us will benefit if it does. As it is, too many well-intentioned people and too many well-intentioned institutions are forced to scrounge for scraps of funding wherever they can find them. What we need, as a friend who works for a large foundation told me, is money that, however dirty its sources, will help to hold utilitarian necessity at bay so that other things can flourish.

ENDNOTES

PROLOGUE

1 *The Onion*: June 22, 2025, Vol 61, Special Edition.

2 Shane Goldmacher, "Democrats Are Still Searching for Path Out of the Wilderness," *The New York Times*, May 26, 2025, p A9.

3 Shane Goldmacher, "A 12-Year Slide to the Right in Nearly Every Corner of America," *The New York Times*, May 31, 2025, A12–13.

4 Angelina Giannopoulou, "Be Like Greta Thunberg," *Transform/ Europe*, June 4, 2025, and "Rich kids of Europe? Social basis and strategic choices in the climate activism of Fridays for Future," *Donatella della Porta* and *Martín Portos, Italian Political Science Review / Rivista Italiana di Scienza Politica*, Volume 53 Issue 1, March 2023, pp. 24–49. Thanks to my colleague Shamus Khan, author of *Privilege* (2013), for steering me toward this and other relevant sociological research.

5 "Rich kids of Europe? Social basis and strategic choices in the climate activism of Fridays for Future," Donatella della Porta and Martín Portos, *Italian Political Science Review / Rivista Italiana di Scienza Politica,* Volume 53 Issue 1, March 2023 , pp. 24–49.

6 What check your privilege means in common usage: "We all carry around privilege of some kind. Simply put, this means that we may, unknowingly, have certain advantages over others. And this is only because there are aspects of our identity that society values over others." "Ever Been Told to Check Your Privilege? Here's What That Really Means." Sam Dylan Finch, *Everyday Feminism*, July 27, 2015.

7 For a subtly nuanced account of the historical intersection of interests between black power and the US financial elite, see

Karen Ferguson, *Top Down: The Ford Foundation, Black Power, and the Reinvention of Racial Liberalism*. Philadelphia, University of Pennsylvania Press, 2013.

8 Frank Parkin, (New York: Praeger, 1968).

WHAT DO ELITES LIVE ON?

1 Christophe Charle, *Birth of the Intellectuals 1880–1900* (Polity, 2015).

2 "Si Gérard n'a pas été riche, c'est qu'il ne l'a pas voulu et qu'il a dédaigné de l'être" (12). Clément Borgal, *De Quoi Vivait Gérard de Nerval*. Paris: Deux Rives, 1950.

3 Nerval (1808–1855) inherited 30,000 francs in 1834 from his maternal grandfather. He was 26. The equivalent of about \$1,000,000 to \$2,000,000 today. Borgal questions the story or stories about him inheriting—at least from a supposed uncle. In any case, he passed for a dandy living on an inheritance whether he had received the inheritance or not!

4 Pierre Bourdieu, *The Rules of Art: Genesis and Structure of the Literary Field*. Trans. Susan Emanuel. Stanford: Stanford University Press, 1996. The French version came out in 1992. Bohemia also figures prominently in *The Field of Cultural Production: Essays on Art and Literature*. Trans. Randal Johnson. NY: Columbia University Press, 1993, which collects essays from the previous decade.

5 Peter Sloterdijk, *Critique of Cynical Reason*. Trans. Michael Eldred. Foreword by Andreas Huyssen. Minneapolis: University of Minnesota Press, 1987. Helen Small, *The Function of Cynicism at the Present Time* (Oxford: Oxford University Press, 2020).

6 The cynical sociologist, like Eyal, would say that no one represents the general or common interest; everyone just represents themselves and their self-interest.

7 Steven Kelman, *Push Comes to Shove: The Escalation of Student Protest*. Boston: Houghton Mifflin, 1970.

8 Paul Berman, *A Tale of Two Utopias: The Political Journey of the Generation of 1968*. NY: Norton, 1996, 36.

9 Musa al-Gharbi, We Have Never been Woke: The Cultural Contradictions of a New Elite. Princeton UP, 2024.

For al-Gharbi, for example, the anti-war movement never had anything to do with what the US bombers were doing to the Vietnamese. The cause was Lyndon Johnson ending student exemptions. Notice the italics: "*This* led to the nation-wide student protest movement" (88). One can concede the difference it made to have a draft, or no draft, in comparing the strength of the protests against US wars in Afghanistan and Iraq and still insist that there were indeed anti-war movements without a draft and recoil with mild surprise at the absolutism: it's *this*, meaning it's not that, not that at all. For al-Gharbi, inspired by Bourdieu, students are "symbolic capitalists." Their aim is symbolic profit. In the Depression, protesters were "aspiring elites," and their "core demands" were "largely self-oriented" (84). The only choice is between being perfectly altruistic, unconcerned with their own futures, and being totally self interested, unconcerned in the slightest for those in whose name they were demonstrating.

10 Indeed, cynicism about the protests was perhaps more attractive to defenders of Israel than Zionism itself, since Zionism obliged them to assume, in defiance of moral decency, that "any violence committed by Palestinians justifies all violence by Israel, and no violence committed by Israel justifies any by Palestinians." Tom Stevenson, "Illusions of Containment," a review of *Hamas: The Quest for Power* by Beverley Milton-Edwards and Stephen Farrell, *LRB*, 6 February 2025, 7–10, p 8

11 David Brooks, *Bobos in Paradise: The New Upper Class and How They Got There*. NY: Simon and Schuster, 2000. Brooks eventually backs off: "Intellectual life is a mixture of careerism and altruism" (152). He does not say that for Bourdieu, careerism is limited or that altruism can be genuine.

12 William A. Henry III's *In Defense of Elitism* (NY: Anchor Doubleday, 1994). Anyone interested enough to open Henry's book should also have a look at Joel Stein's humorous-but-serious volume with a longer title: *In Defense of Elitism: Why I'm Better Than You and You Are Better Than Someone Who Didn't Buy This Book* (NY: Grand Central, 2019).

13 David Brooks, "The Sins of the Educated Class," *New York Times*, June 7, 2024, A25

14 Todd Gitlin, *The Sixties: Years of Hope, Days of Rage*. New York: Bantam, 1993 [1987], 308.

15 It is because the protesters are an elite, and not because they care about the poor, that they are constantly taking positions against privilege, as if to show that they are not themselves privileged. Why they could not simply enjoy their privilege, free of any guilt, is not a question Brooks asks.

16 Reflecting on Raymond Aron's sociological takedown of Sartre and other Marxisant intellectuals in *The Opium of the Intellectuals*, Bourdieu professes to name this trap and thus avoid it: "Aron makes no attempt to ask himself from what point of view he operates this sovereign objectification . . . trapped within the lights of his self-interest, he is entirely blind, as blind as those whose blindness he denounces…" Pierre Bourdieu, *Homo Academicus*, trans. Peter Collier. Stanford: Stanford University Press, 1988, xvi.

17 Lewis A. Coser, *Men of Ideas: A Sociologists's View*. New York: Free Press, 1970.

18 See, however, the evidence for the significant policy impact of the peace movement assembled by David Cortright in *A Chorus of Defiance*, *Boston Review*, April 24, 2025, https://www.bostonreview.net/articles/a-chorus-of-defiance/

19 Louis Menand, "Strong Opinions," *The New Yorker*, June 2, 2025, 55.

20 When a sociologist argues that opposition to the social order is coming from the privileged, and not from the unprivileged, which is where the non-sociologist would expect it to be coming, the argument is also making another, less obvious point: That sociology deserves to exist, that the discipline makes a valuable contribution to public knowledge and deserves to be funded. It's proof of disciplinary value added, as when historians demonstrate (it's a signature move) that a given action or event has had "unintended consequences." There is no scandal in this. Disciplines need to make a case for their existence and keep making it.

21 Sociology has tried to extend its jurisdiction as well as defend it from intrusions. There is nothing scandalous about this. Antagonism is the norm for disciplines.

22 Gil Eyal, *The Origins of Postcommunist Elites: From Prague Spring to the Breakup of Czechoslovakia* (Minneapolis: University of Minnesota Press, 2003). Eyal argues that the breakup of Czechoslovakia was the result of infighting between various "class fractions," which is to say a struggle for power between different elites (xxiii), each elite representing its own local interests. More interestingly, Eyal also concludes that the cynical model is self-contradictory: "[I]t is precisely when postcommunist actors are the most 'cynical,' precisely when they pursue their own interests and political strategies, they cannot help but reproduce the whole set of relations and oppositions composing the intraclass struggle" (199).

23 Here I am responding to the famous Wilt Chamberlain argument for clean, or just, economic rewards in Robert Nozick's *Anarchy, State, and Utopia*. NY: Basic Books, 1975.

24 One example of moralizing about making a living in the domain of art is Bernard Williams in his reflections on Gauguin. Williams is justly fascinated by the idea that, if a decision to pursue art might be justifiable only retroactively by the achievement of artistic success, it would defy moral principles in the moment when it was made.

25 Doug Henwood, "Take Me to Your Leader: The Rot of the American Ruling Class," *Jacobin*, April 27, 2021. https://jacobin.com/2021/04/take-me-to-your-leader-the-rot-of-the-american-ruling-class

26 Steve Fraser and Gary Gerstle recognize the historical existence of "numerous kinds of elites" but choose as most significant, similarly, "those elites who sought to use their economic wealth to achieve national political power" (16). Steve Fraser and Gary Gerstle, eds., *Ruling America: A History of Wealth and Power in a Democracy*. Cambridge: Harvard University Press, 2005.

27 https://www.urban.org/sites/default/files/2024-11/Measur-

ing-the-True-Cost-of-Economic-Security.pdf. The figures drawn from here are from 2022.

28 Madeline Leung Coleman, "How Many New Yorkers are Secretly Subsidized by their Parents?" *New York Magazine*, February 10, 2025. https://nymag.com/intelligencer/article/boomer-generation-wealth-nyc-how-do-people-afford-to-live.html

29 Walter Benn Michaels, *The Trouble with Diversity: How We Learned to Love Identity and Ignore Diversity*. New York: Metropolitan Books, 2006. "Walter Benn Michaels teaches at the University of Illinois, Chicago. He makes $175,000 a year. But he wants more; one of his motives for writing this book was the cash advance offered him by his publishers. Some readers will be tempted to see a discrepancy between these facts and the arguments against economic inequality made in the preceding chapters. But they should remember that those arguments are true (if they are true) even if Michaels's motives are bad, and they would be false (even if they were false) even if his motives were good. Not to put too fine a point on it, the validity of the arguments does not depend on the virtue of the person making them" (191).

30 "The average landlord is a 58-year-old individual, with a median income (not including rent) of £24,000. Karl Marx and Adam Smith once agreed that almost everybody's interests—workers, industrialists, governments—were aligned against landlords. Yet today most of us, even those of us who rent, are no more than a few degrees of separation away from a rentier." Jack Shenker, "Renters vs Rentiers," *The London Review of Books*, May 8, 2025, 22.

31 This "simple state of affairs," Weber writes, "has very frequently been decisive for the role the class situation has played in the formation of political parties. For example, it has made possible the varieties of patriarchal socialism and the frequent attempts . . . of threatened status groups to form alliances with the proletariat against the 'bourgeoisie'" (186). That is roughly the opposite of what has been happening recently in the United

States. It is the business executives who have formed alliances with the working class, and it is the "status groups," including academics and other experts, at whom the ill will of the working class has been directed.

32 Scott Lucas, *The Betrayal of Dissent: Beyond Orwell, Hitchens and the New American Century*. London: Pluto, 2004 mentions Richard Rees, Baronet, one of the rich men whose money made Orwell's career possible as an "independent" writer, along with Victor Gollancz, Sir Stafford Cripps, and George Strauss, a wealthy metal merchant turned parliamentarian who was co-founder of the socialist newspaper *Tribune*.

AT LEAST MODERN COMFORT

1 One reason for *not* asking such questions might of course be a desire to respect the ambition and the accomplishment. The insistence on asking indicates at least a willingness to contemplate a less respectful attitude.

2 Michael Bérubé, "The Blessed of the Earth," *Social Text* No. 49, The Yale Strike Dossier (Winter, 1996), pp. 75-95, https://www.jstor.org/stable/i220079. A decade or so later, when Yale teaching assistants were protesting, Amy Hungerford, then at Yale, now Executive Vice President of Columbia, wrote an op-ed saying, in effect, that they were spoiled brats who had no right to the means of protest like the hunger strike that might be proper for *real* victims of injustice.

3 Paul Jacobs and Saul Landau, *The New Radicals*. New York: Pelican, 1966.

4 Richard Flacks, "The Liberated Generation: An Exploration of the Roots of Student Protest," *Journal of Social Issues*, 23:3 (1967), 52-75.

5 Todd Gitlin, *The Sixties: Years of Hope, Days of Rage*. New York: Bantam, 1993 [1987]. As Gitlin notes, "Affluence, already a well-established Fifties term when John Kenneth Galbraith published *The Affluent Society* in 1958, "was far more American than 'rich,' harnessed as that brutal syllable is to its natural

counterpart, 'poor,' thus bringing inequality to mind. 'Affluence' sounds general, and in the Fifties it was assumed to be a national condition, not just a personal standing" (12).

6 "The fact that the Statement was drafted at a labor education camp was hardly a fluke. In the early 1960s Walter Reuther and the coterie of ex-socialists and frustrated radicals that advised him were desperate to break out of the political and organizational straitjacket into which big labor had been drawn during the previous twenty years. As Nelson Lichtenstein makes clear, there were a remarkable number of parallels between the programmatic initiatives proposed in the Statement and the kind of resolutions that the United Auto Workers (UAW) leadership wrote and passed at their union conventions. The Reutherites therefore welcomed this new generation of campus-based radicals and funded several SDS educational and organizing projects" (8-9). Richard Flacks and Nelson Lichtenstein, eds., *The Port Huron Statement: Sources and Legacies of the New Left's Founding Manifesto.* Philadelphia: University of Pennsylvania Press, 2015. On UAW funding, see also p. 23.

7 Alexander Cockburn, "Introduction," in *Student Power: Problems, Diagnosis, Action*, edited by Alexander Cockburn and Robin Blackburn. London: Penguin in association with New Left Review, 1969, p 7.

8 Immanuel Wallerstein, *University in Turmoil: The Politics of Change.* New York: Atheneum, 1969. See my "Student Power," *The New Statesman*, May 11, 2024. Students can legitimately try to shift the center leftwards. That would include achieving some reform in the governance of the university itself, including curbing its misconduct as a property owner, and taking some steps toward racial equality. They might even get (on the model of certain European universities) an administration elected by the faculty. In order not to endanger such projects and accomplishments, the left should beware of extremist language. Wallerstein gives advice: "any tactic that cuts off

communication of the left with the center (the latter being the majority of university professors, large segments of the professional classes, most skilled workers) is self-defeating" (137).

9 Grace Elizabeth Hale, "The Romance of Rebellion" in Flacks and Lichtenstein.

10 Paul Berman, *A Tale of Two Utopias: The Political Journey of the Generation of 1968*. NY: Norton, 1996, p. 32.

11 Franco Moretti, *The Bourgeois: Between History and Literature*. London: Verso, 2013.

12 According to data from the Hope Center for College, Community, and Justice, approximately 18–20% of all college students, including graduate students, have been found to use SNAP (that is, food stamps) or qualify for it due to food insecurity. And many more would qualify. https://hope.temple.edu/policy-advocacy/gao-confirms-what-we-already-know-students-face-unacceptable-food-insecurity. See also the previous results of US General Accountability Office (GAO) and Hope Center surveys of food insecurity, https://hope.temple.edu/npsas. On student debt, see Andrew Ross, *Creditocracy and the Case for Debt Refusal*. New York: OR Books, 2013. It cannot be forgotten that student debt has been an enormous source of profit in the financial industry, which is to say that it has contributed to many trust funds.

13 Caitlin Zaloom, *Indebted: How Families Make College Work at Any Cost*. Princeton: Princeton University Press, 2019.

14 Christopher Hayes, *The Twilight of the Elites: America After Meritocracy* NY: Broadway, 2012.

15 Christophe Guilluy, *Twilight of the Elites: Prosperity, the Periphery, and the Future of France*, trans. Malcolm Debevoise, Yale UP, 2019. The book was originally published in France in 2016 without the word elites in the title—the French title has "d'en haut," from above.

16 Catherine Liu, *Virtue Hoarders: The Case Against the Professional Managerial Class*. Minneapolis: University of Minnesota Press, 2021.

17 Michael M. Grynbaum, *Empire of the Elite: Inside Condé Nast, the Media Dynasty That Reshaped America*, New York: Simon and Schuster, 2025.

18 This story is told in greater detail by Thomas Frank in *The Conquest of Cool: Business Culture, Counterculture, and the Rise of Hip Consumerism*. Chicago: University of Chicago Press, 1997. Brooks does not cite this book. Frank too discredits the counterculture by asserting that the culture no longer counters the bourgeoisie, if it ever did. Brooks argues, more precisely, that the bourgeois bohemians discovered a resolution or balance between the two decades and the two sides in the culture war.

19 Evidence that "birth," whether as sign of noble blood or the possession of material wealth, has not disappeared comes from the editorial board of *Who's Who,* which "stands by the book's original intention, to recognize people whose '*prominence is inherited*, or depending upon office, or the result of ability which singles them out from their fellows in occupations open to every educated man or woman'" (my italics; J Parry, 19). They too draw on Bourdieu, whom they seem to understand as seeing artistic/intellectual distinction ending up in monetary reward. Jonathan Parry, "Snobs, Swots and Hacks," LRB, 23 January 2025, 19-20. A review of *Born to Rule: The Making and Remaking of the British Elite*, Aaron Reeves and Sam Friedman, Harvard, 2024.

20 David N. Smith, *Who Rules the Universities? An Essay in Class Analysis*. NY: Monthly Review Press, 1974.

21 On the foundational thinkers (Italian and French) in sociology and political theory who developed the concept of the elite, see Geraint Parry, *Political Elites*. NY: Praeger, 1969. Parry defines elites as "small minorities who appear to play an exceptionally influential part in political and social affairs" (13). As he recognizes, the real subject when elites are discussed is power (14) and whether power "is in the hands of a cohesive, self-conscious minority" (14).

22 See Christopher Hayes, *Twilight of the Elites: America After Meritocracy*. New York: Broadway, 2012.

23 Christophe Charle, *Birth of the Intellectuals 1880-1900* (Polity, 2015). The birth of the intellectuals comes out of a "contradiction between the official values of the Republic (meritocracy, the cult of great men who embodied the national spirit) and the actual laws of reproduction of its elites" (6). The actuality included "the growing weight of relations of economic dependence in cultural production" (7). "The justification of their power was ... perfectly circular: in a still rural society, only those who enjoyed a certain affluence had access to knowledge; that affluence afforded them the leisure to devote themselves to public affairs, while higher education legitimized their capacity to lead" (49). This "apparently flawless syllogism" (49)—still going strong in Weber—is wrong, Charle says, in the sense that "power had too often been confiscated by the wealthiest or those privileged by birth to the detriment of the most enlightened" (49).

24 In France at the end of the nineteenth century, Charle informs us, the leaders of the right anticipated Helen Small's argument that the highly educated cannot claim to be essential to the social whole; the words of the humanists, they complained, do not reach enough of society. Better than the humanistically educated, the right argued, was leadership by the military, which with universal conscription "educated the whole nation" (188).

25 Fritz K. Ringer, The Decline of the German Mandarins: The German Academic Community, 1890-1933. Hanover: University Press of New England, [1969] 1990.

26 Mike Savage, "Introduction to Elites: From the "Problematic of the Proletariat" to a class analysis of 'wealth elites,'" *The Sociological Review*, 2015, Vol 63, pp 223-239.

27 Michael Sandel, *Tyranny of Meritocracy* (2021).

28 Christopher Lasch, *The Revolt of the Elites and the Betrayal of Democracy*. NY: Norton, 1995.

29 Even the robber barons who ended up funding so many museums, libraries, universities, and foundations might be surprised to hear that the motives and consequences of their profit-making were so profoundly ethical.

30 Andrew Delbanco, *College: What It Was, Is, and Should Be*. Second Edition. Princeton, 2012/ 2023.

31 See "The Impossible Math of Philanthropy," Hans Taparia and Bruce Buchanan. *New York Times*, Feb. 3, 2025.

32 See Antonio Y. Vásquez-Arroyo, *Political Responsibility: Responding to Predicaments of Power*. New York: Columbia University Press, 2016.

33 See also the references to the service ethic in the Ehrenreich essay on the professional-managerial class.

34 Gabriel Winant, "Professional-Managerial Chasm," *n+1*, October 10, 2019.

35 Barbara and John Ehrenreich, "Death of a Yuppie Dream: The Rise and Fall of the Professional-Managerial Class," Rosa Luxembourg Stiftung, 2013, p. 2–3.

36 On the need for time to read, as a precondition for politics, see Christina Lupton, *Reading and the Making of Time in the Eighteenth Century*. Baltimore and London: Johns Hopkins University Press, 2018.

37 Christopher Lasch: "a 'competence,' as they called it, referred both to property itself and to the intelligence and enterprise required by its management" (7). Lasch is referring to the ideology of the nineteenth-century property-holder. The chapter entitled "A Modest Competency" in Leonore Davidoff and Catherine Hall, *Family Fortunes* (Chicago, 1987) suggests that competency, another word for independence, is a masculine concept, implicitly set off against the assumed dependency of women and children. For Lasch it's an entirely positive term, one which (one might say) whitewashes the ownership of property by merging it with the intelligence needed to manage the property.

38 The neglect of money in attacks on elites gets a weird, backhanded recognition in William A. Henry III's *In Defense of Elitism*, published in the midst of the Culture Wars. Henry criticizes the universities for being anti-elitist, not for being elitists. While indulging in an anti-egalitarian rant that he himself describes as "crank attitudinizing," he notices however that his

egalitarian enemies are not taking exception to the power of money. "Gradually and reluctantly, however, I realized that the wrath directed at elitism has less to do with money than with popular egalitarian scorn for the very kinds of intellectual distinction-making I hold most dear" (2). William A Henry III, *In Defense of Elitism*. NY: Doubleday, 1994. His book should perhaps be served with a portion of Joel Stein's book of the same title (New York: Grand Central Publishing, 2019: the subtitle is "Why I'm Better Than You and You are Better Than Someone Who Didn't Buy This Book"). Conclusions can perhaps be drawn from the fact that both Henry and Stein were writers for *Time Magazine*.

39 Jane Mayer, Dark Money: The Hidden History of the Billionaires Behind the Rise of the Radical Right (New York: Anchor Books, 2017) or Frances Stonor Saunders's The Cultural Cold War: The CIA and the World of Arts and Letters (NY: The New Press, 1999/2013). The British title of Stonor Saunders's book was Who Paid the Piper?

WHAT DO LITTLE MAGAZINES LIVE ON?

1 In class terms, inheritance is a hand-me-down from the aristocracy. It is not the same as selling your labor on the market. An inheritance allows you to defy the market, but only by benefitting from the stored-up market-based labor of others. Its distance from the marketplace, though only relative, translates into a sense of autonomy that is continuous with the aristocracy's traditional contempt for labor. The place Bourdieu assigns to inherited money helps explain the dandyism of the nineteenth-century bohemians; think of Nerval taking his pet lobster for a walk. In this sense if not in others, to insult academics as a new aristocracy is not just loose speech.

2 Max Weber, *Charisma and Disenchantment: The Vocation Lectures*. Ed. Paul Reiter and Chad Wellmon, trans. Damion Searles. NY: New York Review Books, 2020.

3 I am happy to acknowledge a longstanding debt here to Fredric

Jameson, "The Vanishing Mediator; or, Max Weber as Storyteller," Fredric Jameson, *The Ideologies of Theory, Essays 1971-1986, Volume 2, Syntax of History*. Minneapolis: University of Minnesota Press, 1988, 3–34.

4 Lutz Kaelber, "How Well Do We Know Max Weber After All? A New Look at Max Weber and His Anglo-German Family Connections," *International Journal of Politics, Culture, and Society*, 17:2 (Winter 2003), 307–327. Kaelber is reviewing Guenther Roth's *Max Webers deutsch-englische Familiengeschichte, 1800-1950. Mit Briefen und Dokumenten* [Max Weber's German-English Family History. With Letters and Documents].

5 Wendy Brown, *Nihilistic Times: Thinking with Max Weber*. Cambridge: Harvard University Press, 2023.

6 The sums involved must have been significant even before Tanner moved on to luxury watches and other jewelry. In 1981 O.C. Tanner benefited from an addition to the Economic Recovery Tax Act, which drastically reduced the rates on business income. Less well known, it increased the tax deduction for employee recognition awards. But the lecture series had already been endowed in 1978, the lectures to be given in six universities, so that would not have mattered very much.

7 Antonio Y. Vázquez-Arroyo, *Political Responsibility: Responding to Predicaments of Power*. New York: Columbia University Press, 2016.

8 Berman's account of protest as groundless, morally disinterested action-at-a-distance is precarious but heroic. On the other hand, it sets the movement up for inevitable failure, not because radical solidarity with distant others can't work but because eventually the protesters will take up their own cause, will become self-interested. The name of this turn, for him, is identity politics. "The idea had been to take privileged young people and put them on the side of the oppressed. On someone else's side, not their own. On the side of people who needed help. But the argument for feminism and gay liberation said, in effect, that in the student world everybody was not, on closer inspection, so wonderfully

privileged. On the contrary! Whole groups of the comfortable middle class—the women, the homosexuals, and by extension anybody at all who suffered from historic prejudices—were suddenly revealed to have grievances of their own" (118). Self-interest takes over, and that is the movement's downfall.

9 Lennard J. Davis, *Poor Things: How Those with Money Depict Those without It*. Durham: Duke University Press, 2024.

10 The story of how Brooks talked his way into that job offer is amusingly told in Mary Ruth Yoe, "Everybody's a Critic". University of Chicago Magazine. (February 2004).

11 https://www.immigrantentrepreneurship.org/entries/henry-miller-the-cattle-king-of-california/

12 Kaiser, Charles (May 11, 2024). "Morning After the Revolution review: a bad faith attack on 'woke'". *The Guardian*. Retrieved June 12, 2025.

13 As the reader is perhaps already thinking, this paradox can perhaps be broken down into non-contradictory elements. Not all intellectuals see themselves as adversarial, nor are they so seen by those around them. This is even truer for academics. Society may be making a perfectly rational investment in a group whose labors uphold the status quo. Still, "critical thinking," a staple in unreadable university mission statements, comes closer to "social criticism" than to, say, "potentially profitable innovation." The innocent-sounding definition of the intellectual as more properly "public" than "oppositional," as presumed for example by Stefan Collini, arguably contains more political opposition—to the private, to the authority of the market—than it may seem to. Another way of resolving this apparent paradox: to break down "society" into different parts, which are presumably pulling in different directions. On that assumption, it's one section of society that's adversarial to another section of society; it's not society at war with itself. Presto, no contradiction. Also, there's a need to break down the meanings of "adversarial."

14 The academicization-of-the-intellectuals narrative is taken up again by Russell Jacoby in *The Last Intellectuals: American Culture*

in the Age of Academe (NY: Basic Books, 1987). I worry about the added decline element of this argument (which is not in Coser), in *Intellectuals: Politics, Aesthetics, Academics* (Minneapolis: University of Minnesota Press, 1990), in part by asking how the supposedly independent or detached intellectuals ever made a living. In *Secular Vocations: Intellectuals, Professionalism, Culture (London: Verso, 1993)*, I argue that making a living, like other professionals, though at a lower pay scale, is not a betrayal of the mission or essence of progressive commitments or intellectual labor. It's not lost on me that the present essay is trying to resuscitate those perhaps outdated concerns.

15 Bruce Robbins, Introduction, Bruce Robbins, ed., *Intellectuals: Aesthetics, Politics, Academics*. Minneapolis: University of Minnesota Press, 1990.

16 *What Was the Hipster? A Sociological Investigation*. Ed. Mark Greif, Kathleen Ross, and Dayna Tortorici, transcribed by Avner Davis. New York: n+1 Books, Harper Collins, 2013. *What Was the Hipster?* locates itself at the moment when "a word that has been used for insult and abuse [has been] gaining a neutral or even positive estimation in the culture." Compare with Brooks's story of the bourgeois bohemian.

17 "The work of sociology just about everyone discussed in these pages ought to read and experience, as a kind of required generational exercise in self-criticism, is Pierre Bourdieu's *Distinction* (1979)." (Introduction) Bourdieu will teach (apropos of hipsters, or in general?) that "everyone is trying to distinguish themselves from other people in increasingly trivial ways, thus taking their eye off of essential matters" (Greif in Discussion). There has reportedly been some disagreement over Bourdieu within the ranks of *n+1*'s editors.

18 If you Google "trust fund hipster," which sounds like an open invitation to more or less justified resentment and rage, what you get includes surprisingly positive stuff, like macho stories of hard living with awful insufficient jobs and with roommates in

gross spaces, but "okay" because it was only temporary, a stage of life.

19 In this volume, hipsters are always other people. In *Absent Minds*, Stefan Collini notices much the same phenomenon of disaffiliation in the case of the term "intellectual," which is repeatedly seen to flourish in some other country or period, but rarely here and now.

20 Keith Gessen writes: "In issue 3, our discovery was J. D. Daniels, who'd written us a furious denunciatory letter from Boston about the first issue, then produced a taut, angry piece about rich white kids affecting the fashions of poor white people in the form of "wifebeaters" and trucker hats. "When you wear the Fordson tractor belt buckle my father gave me, you're a hipster," the piece began. "When I wear it, I'm a redneck." "Now we had opened a front in a game we couldn't win: a class war against ourselves." Keith Gessen, "On *n*+1," in Ian Morris and Joanne Diaz, eds., *The Little Magazine in Contemporary America*. Chicago: University of Chicago Press, 2015, 46.

21 The American Revolution came about in part because the colonists were hungry for more and more Native American land and the British crown, unwilling to commit the troops necessary to protect them from the people whose lands they were seizing, told them to stop.

22 Mark Greif, personal communication.

23 T. S. Eliot had "secure backing" from Faber and Faber for *Criterion*, as F. R. Leavis knew (15). His ambition to make *Scrutiny* something like such American journals as *Sewanee Review* had no such backing. The money came from the sale of a terrace house Leavis had bought in Leys Road in 1929 for about £1,000 (145). That would be about £83,000 today. Ian MacKillop, *F.R. Leavis: A Life in Criticism*. London: Allen Lane, 1995.

24 Lou Anne Bulik, *Mass Culture Criticism and* Dissent, *an American Socialist Magazine*. Bern, Peter Lang, 1993. Bulik 57-58. "Unlike its two closest competitors at the time, *Partisan Review* and *Com-*

mentary, Dissent did not pay its editorial staff and contributors for their work. In the beginning, one of the editors contributed a spare bedroom closet to house the subscription lists, and the editorial meetings took place in various apartments. Maurice Isserman, *If I Had a Hammer: The Death of the Old Left and the Birth of the New Left*. New York: Basic Books, 1987, (10). Bulik quotes Walzer: It was "run like a little grocery store" (73n2). They decided not to launch until they had enough money to guarantee one year of publication.

25 https://en.wikipedia.org/wiki/Joseph_Buttinger.

26 For a scathing though probably not representative take on university trustees, see David N. Smith, *Who Rules the Universities? An Essay in Class Analysis*. NY: Monthly Review Press, 1974. Starting from the premise that "the University of California is controlled by a powerful and wealthy Board of Regents, which rules in its own interest," he goes on to find them typical of university trustees (14). The fact that capitalism now requires educated workers doesn't mean, Smith argues, that it's not capitalism or that the educated workers, whose culture and attitudes have changed along with their incomes, are not still, structurally, workers, even if better paid, at least some of them.

27 Terry A. Cooney's *The Rise of the New York Intellectuals*: Partisan Review and Its Circle, 1934–1945. Madison: University of Wisconsin Press, 1986.

28 Saunders, 282 and passim.

29 In fiscal year 2023, 12.6% of U.S. residents, or 42.1 million people per month, received benefits from the Supplemental Nutrition Assistance Program (SNAP). However, the percentage of people receiving SNAP varies by state, ranging from 4.6% in Utah to 23.1% in New Mexico.

30 Duncan Thompson, Pessimism of the Intellect?: A History of the New Left Review, London: Merlin Press, 2006.

31 Sebastian Budgen, an editor at Verso, reports that in his opinion money was not decisive. Personal communication.

32 Benedict Anderson, *A Life Beyond Boundaries: A Memoir.* London: Verso, 2016.

33 New York State Council of the Arts,

34 Gessen, 44.

35 Lewis Coser, *Men of Ideas: A Sociologist's View.* NY: The Free Press, 1965/1970. "Intellect ... presumes a capacity for detachment from immediate experience, a moving beyond the pragmatic tasks of the moment" (viii).

36 Wallerstein's analysis of the student protests of the 60s confirms the basic structure of common interest between the ethnic poor, recipients of social services, and the educated middle class, who are employed providing those services. "To the extent that the expansion of urban public-service enterprises increases service to the urban ethnic lower classes, the money expended meets both sets of demands" (54).

37 "Contrary to their radical rhetoric," al-Gharbi writes, the student protesters "wanted relatively high-status jobs and socioeconomically comfortable lives far more than they wanted to *actually* overthrow the existing order" (85). This is the pseudo-academic equivalent of a Trumpian rant. No statistics are given to support the assertions about what the protesters really want. How does al-Gharbi know the things he asserts? How can he possibly know *how much* student protesters want social justice, *how much* they want "high-status jobs," so as to be able to compare these quantities? Sociology is supposed to be serious about its statistics and about the testing of its hypotheses. (Al-Gharbi is currently employed as a teacher of journalism, so perhaps he is no longer aspiring to write within the discipline of sociology.) Artists and writers, students and professors have much the same desire for comfort and security that everyone else has. Has al-Gharbi weighed his assertions against, say, the hypothesis that (as they might well say if asked) what the student protesters really want is to inhabit a social order in which both the protesters and everyone else would enjoy "socioeconomically comfortable lives"?

38 Speaking of taxes, writers, and the inherited funds that facilitated careers in writing, it is worth mentioning the number of writers whose fathers were tax collectors. They include Racine (1639-1699), Voltaire (1694-1778), Hugo (1802–1885), and Stendhal (1783-1842). The profession could often be more precisely described as tax farming, a private enterprise, contracted out but with the coercive power of the state behind it, by which personal fortunes were accumulated. For obvious reasons tax farming lent itself to abuse. It is cited as a cause of the French Revolution.

BOURDIEU AND TAXES

1 See Jon Wiener, "The Olin Money Tree: Dollars for Neocon Scholars," *The Nation*, Jan 1, 1990, 12–13.

2 The founding of the *Fondation* and its history until 1994 are recounted in Emmanuelle Pavillon, *La Fondation de France: 1969–1994 : l'invention d'un mécénat contemporain*. Paris: Anthropos, 1995. The story continues in Brigitte Broca's *La Fondation de France 1994-2008*. np: Perrin, 2009.

3 Gérard de Nerval, Oeuvres completes, Volume 9, ed. Jacques-Remi Dahan. Paris: Classiques Garnier, 2015.

EPILOGUE

1 For the publication history of Chomsky's essay, "The Responsibility of Intellectuals," whose understanding of privilege has been an inspiration to me, see Robin D.G. Kelley, "The Responsibility of Intellectuals in the Age of Fascism and Genocide," *Boston Review*, 2025.3, 6–25.

BRUCE ROBBINS is the Old Dominion Foundation Professor in the Humanities at Columbia University.